ited

ca

COUNTY LIBRARY

TRAVELS IN THE UNITED STATES OF AMERICA;

Commencing in the Year 1793, and Ending in 1797. With The
Author's Journals of his Two Voyages Across the Atlantic

BY WILLIAM PRIEST, Musician, Late of the Theatres Philadelphia,
Baltimore and Boston.

CAPPRICCIO con — —

1802.

PREFACE.

An elegant writer observes that a preface may be dispensed with in any work, if the author (either from his humility of justice) think that his style be calculated only to put his readers to sleep. Though I do not think the publication of the following sheets will *materially* affect the price of opium, I cannot intrude this volume on the public without informing them, what all my friends will vouch for the truth of, viz. — that on my return from America, in 1797, I wrote the work in its present form *for their* perusal; and, that conscious of my want of talent as a writer, I resisted all their entreaties for its publication, till within these three months.

The public, I presume, will not be *wholly* disappointed; the *extracts* I have made from *Jefferson*, *Belknap*, and other american writers, are worthy their attention: *I* have no other merit than having placed them in a tolerable point of view.

"The God of Truth, and all who know
me, will bear testimony that, from my
whole soul, I despise deceit, as I do all
silly claims to superior wisdom, and
infallibility, which so many writers, by
a thousand artifices, endeavour to make
their readers imagine they possess."

CONTENTS.

PENNSYLVANIA PLANTER—enjoys a happy state of mediocrity between riches and poverty—the children how disposed of—the boys—effect of the religious education given to the girls not intirely eradicated even by a brothel—a country sleighing match—another in Philadelphia in stile—a fiddler a necessary apendage

FROGS—two extracts—they sit croaking to the wonderment of strangers— land of enchantment—frog concert—how supported— treble—counter tenor— tenor—bass—fire-flies—night-hawks— probable effects on an enthusiastic cockney

JOURNEY TO LANCASTER—the Pioli—Wayne's surprise— appointed to the command of the western army—Indian war— shocking effects of— misunderstanding between the Canadians and American citizens—accounted for—French agents—the British government vindicated—Proceed on the journey—charming prospects—beauties of the Susquana destroys the navigation— arrival at Lancaster—rifle manufactory—uncommon shot of two back woodsmen—Dutch schools—three concerts—two German sans culottes— extracts from the regulations of the Hanover dancing assembly—German and Irish emigrants

FEDERAL COINAGE not approved of by the people—the new scheme contrasted with the old one—advantages of an even division by the decimal

DELAWARE SHAD FISHERY—stupidity of the Anglo-Americans in giving English names to animals peculiar to the new continent— length of the siens— greatest haul of shad on record—fanatical law of the Quakers injurious to the fishery—sturgeon—extract from general Lincoln on the migration of fishes

JOURNEY TO BALTIMORE—water-stage—Newcastle—Glasgow— the Elk—bay of Chesapeake—arrival at Baltimore—yellow fever

BALTIMORE—situation—disadvantages of—the Dutch plan of canals not adapted to a southern latitude—the former race-course in the centre of the town—anecdote

MANUFACTORIES—not the interest of the Americans to engage in them—why— American iron—its malleability—two patents granted by Congress— sawing-mills—ship-building

SHOOTING AND FISHING—partridges—no game laws—woodcocks in August—the American ortolan—back woodsmen—their game—wild turkey—squirrel shooting—American fishing parties—how conducted

INDIANS—genius for oratory, painting, and sculpture—their continence— extract—the Indian student—the splenetic Indian—his remedy—seen in another point of view—the Indian orator—verses on an Indian burial-ground

SCHEME OF A RIFLE CORPS—of forming the corps—rifles—powder— accoutrements and dress—exercise

SPECULATION—the United States—the land of—100 acres of land for a dollar—flour—the mines—description of a coal-bank

CLIMATE—Cooper on this subject not to be depended upon—quotation from Jefferson—the N. W. wind not accounted for—Volney—his intended investigation

WHITE SLAVE TRADE—mortality on board a white Guineaman from Ireland— Hibernian and German societies—the trade not allowed in New England—a German flesh-butcher sells his countrymen at Philadelphia during the fatal yellow fever of 1793

JOURNEY TO BOSTON—Pennsylvania the garden of the United States— Bristol—Trentown—New Brunswick—New York—arrival in Yankee Land—land speculators harangue—interrupted—arrival at Boston—P. S.—dramatic mania—detestation of the primitive Bostonians to theatricals—are first introduced as moral lectures—the theatrical opposition

BATTLE OF BUNKER'S HILL—inscription from a monument on the scene of action—anecdotes of Cox, the celebrated bridge-architect—connects Boston with the Continent—goes to Ireland, where he builds seven bridges

BOSTON—situation—West Boston—advantages of the harbour—the long wharf—new theatre—university of Cambridge—new bridge a mile in length— Irish market

BOSTONIAN FIRE ALARM—amateur firemen—negro incendiaries—good effects of their villainy

FANATICISM—Brownists—intolerance proved from their own writers— rebellion against parents made a capital crime—smoking tobacco and drinking healths forbidden—proclamation against wearing long hair— persecution of the Quakers—Penn's retaliation—poetry

NEGRO SLAVERY—state of in the Southern, Middle, and New England Slates— abolition society—extract from Jefferson's Virginia

YELLOW FEVER—a new disorder—first imported from the coast of Guinea to the West Indies in 1792—extract from Dr. Rush—a disorder fatal only to one race of men not new—plague among the red men—how accounted for by the fanatics—not to the satisfaction of a philosopher—age of the world proved to be 36,960 years from the falls of Niagara

AMERICAN FISHERY ON THE BANKS OK NEWFOUNDLAND— extract from Dr. Belknap— dumb fish—how cured—merchantable— Jamaica fish—former and present state of the fishery

NEW ENGLAND STATES COMPARED WITH THOSE OF THE SOUTH—beauty of the women— accounted for—general knowledge of the inhabitants—free schools—how supported— difference of climate

VOYAGE TO ENGLAND—journal—severe gale at N. E.—the vessel encrusted with ice—stand to the southward—the gulph stream— another gale—misfortunes— arrival at Dover—conclusion

*TRAVELS IN AMERICA. *

London, May 7th, 1797.

DEAR SIR,

Since my return, my friends have made a thousand inquiries respecting the state of America. I do not know how I can inform them of my sentiments on that subject better, than by having the rough draught I preserved of the letters I wrote to you from that country fairly copied for their use. If, like you, they are *really* my friends, they will take the will for the deed. The *truth* of my information, and my *wish* to contribute to their amusement, will be a sufficient apology for the many imperfections they will meet with, in the desultory epistles of

Yours very sincerely.

Annapolis, December 1st, 1793.

DEAR FRIEND,

The enclosed extracts from my journal will I hope convince you, I have not *entirely* forgot my promise at parting. When at Philadelphia I delivered your letters to——. Believe me

Yours very sincerely.

JOURNAL.

Gravesend, on board the George Barclay,

31st of July, 1793.

Arrived onboard at 2 this afternoon, with an intention of sailing to Philadelphia: Gravesend is so called from it's being *the end of a sailors grave*, as those who die on a voyage after passing the fort are thrown over board.

August 1st.

Got under weigh with a light breeze at S. W., which not being sufficient to stem the returning tide, we dropped out anchor again off the Nore light.

Aug. 2nd. —Weighed anchor with the wind at S. E., and on the morning of the 3rd; off Deal, sent a boat on shore, which soon returned with a supply of meat, water, sheep, poultry gin, and gingerbread; dismissed our pilot, and soon after doubted the South Foreland; the prospect of Dover and the adjacent coast delightful.

Aug 8th. —Beating to windward with a fresh breeze off the Lizard; finding it impossible to clear the land, put about, and by three in the afternoon were safe moored in Falmouth harbour. Went on shore; the lower order of the inhabitants chaunt, or rather speak in recitative, a strange dialect, in which I could distinguish several English words.

Took a walk to Pendennis castle, which protects the West entrance of the harbour; found it garrisoned by a party of invalides, who informed me they had not two nights in bed to one up; hard duty after twenty years servitude!

Aug. 9th. —Dined on john dory, which I cannot think equal either to turbot or sole. Falmouth has the best fish market in England: I am informed, in the course of the year, they have upward of fifty different species for sale, on very moderate terms.

Aug. 15th. —Weighed anchor, and having a good breeze at N. E., we were soon clear of the land. On the evening of the 16th came on a smart breeze at S. W.; at 2 A. M. the wind changed to W. N.W. and *blew a hard gale,* which split our jib, and at last obliged us to lie too, under our courses: shipped some very heavy seas over our quarter, which drowned three parts of our stock of geese and other poultry; the baggage of near fifty passengers, for want of being properly lashed, was dashing about the steerage; which, with the shrieks of the women, heaving of the vessel, rattling of the wind, and all the *et cetera* of a storm, was dreadful indeed.

Aug. 18th. —Wind N. W. moderate; the morning delightful; appeared doubly so, contrasted with the horrours of the night.

Aug. 31st. —Fresh breeze at S. W. increasing to a hard gale, reduced us once more to our courses: at 8 P. M. calm, with a very heavy swell.

Sunday 1st September.

Pleasant breeze at N. N.E. The following hymn was written by Mr. Harwood, for this morning's service.

HYMN.

I.

Father of Heav'n, to thee we raise
  (Mark'd by thy kind peculiar care,)
Our songs of thankfulness and praise,
  To thee ascends the grateful pray'r.

II.

Thou didst direct the gentlest breath,
  That o'er the sleeping waters stole;
Thine is the dreadful voice of death,
  In which thy angry thunders roll.

III.

Father of all, 'tis thine to give,
  Not what our erring pray'r demands;
With joy thy blessings we receive,
  And bow submissive 'neath thy hand.

Sept. 7th. —First appearance of the gulf-weed. The trade wind, between the Equator and the extent of the northern Tropic, setting from the eastward, forces the water against the islands, and at length into the gulf of Mexico where it meets with an uniform opposition from the main, causing a strong current to the N. E., or points somewhat in that direction. This stream is so violent as to tear up the sea weeds in the gulf, and bear them as far to the north as latitude 44: the stream is soon after absorbed in the Western ocean; but causes certain counter currents, which, for want of being properly allowed for by mariners, have been the causes of many shipwrecks.

Sept. 8th. —Fine morning; wind at W. S.W. A beautiful dolphin struck at an artificial flying fish, hanging at our bow-sprit; the hook breaking, he escaped; —continued playing round our bows for some time, and struck at several flying fish; but we could not again tempt him with the artificial bait.

Mem. To read this lesson once a month.

Sept. 9th. —Calm and fog, several flocks of wild fowl. Suppose ourselves near the banks of Newfoundland. Thermometer sunk 18 degrees since yesterday.

Sept. 10th. —Pleasant morning, having run to the S. W. during the night: no sign of the banks. A land bird, of the thrush kind, came and settled on our main yard; seemed quite exhausted; fell upon the deck, and was taken up by the cabin boy. The poor creature must have been driven off the coast of America in a violent gale at N. W., the distance from any land being upwards of a thousand miles; no other circumstance could account for it's flying so far.

Sept. 19th. —Wind at N. N.W. very moderate; —the afternoon calm. The sun set this evening with uncommon beauty, that glorious luminary was surrounded with clouds of a vivid yellow, green, and red; strongly shaded with black half the extent of the horizon. The moon at the same time rising to the east-ward, with a cool and faint sky, formed a strong and beautiful contrast.

Sept. 21st. —Wind S. with rain. Caught four dolphins, which afforded us a most delicious repast: in the paunch of one was found a dodon, or globe-fish; the sailors call it a parrot-fish, from its having a beak exactly resembling that bird. —At 9 A. M. spoke with the Queen Charlotte of London, bound to Bristol, out ten days from

Baltimore; the captain's account of the longitude 67. Our joy in being so near the land was of short continuance; for, in one hour after, we spoke with the Union, eight days from Philadelphia. The captain informed us, there was a sort of plague in that city, which carries off great numbers, and that ten thousand of the inhabitants had fled to the country, to avoid the infection.

Sept. 24th. —Soundings at 60 fathom: lay to all night.

Sept. 25th. —Woke with the cry of "Land. " At 10 A. M. we took a pilot on board: he informed us the disorder at Philadelphia is the yellow fever, imported in a french schooner from the West Indies; some of the passengers of this vessel died of this fatal disorder, at a lodging-house in Water-street, and communicated the infection to the family. It is now spreading rapidly through the city, in all directions. The faculty, so far from being able to cure this disorder, have, in several instances, fallen victims to it's fury. Within this few days, a Dr. Rush has discovered this disorder is *not* the yellow fever of the West Indies and has applied an opposite mode of cure by copious bleedings, mercurial medicines, &c. with some success. What is truly extraordinary, the infection does not affect *people of colour!*

Sept. 28th. —Came to an anchor off Glocester Point, five miles below Philadelphia: the vessel proceeds no further at present, as all intercourse with the city is cut off, and business at a stand.

October 1st.

Brought my baggage on shore, and arrived, at four in the afternoon, at Woodbury, the county town of Glocester, in the state of West Jersey. With some difficulty I procured a lodging within half a mile of the town. Woodbury consists of about fifty well built houses, chiefly inhabited by quakers, and other dissenters of the most rigid kind; so very primitive are they in their appearance, that a barber cannot make a living among them.

Oct. 13th. —Spent the last ten days in shooting, and rambling about the woods. The face of the country is exactly that of an immense forest, entirely covered with wood, except the plantation cleared by the settlers. The land sandy, and by no means of a good quality; the chief produce maize, or indian corn. I counted the increase of *one* stalk with three ears; the amount of the grains were upward of *one thousand two hundred*.

Oct. 16th. —I believe the Americans conceive their woods to be inexhaustible. My landlord this day cut down thirty-two young cedars to make a hog-pen. A settler informs me, he raised a gum tree from the seed, which, in sixteen years, measured twenty inches diameter, three feet from it's base. He tells, me they have ten species of oak; viz, white, black, red, spanish, turkey, chesnut, ground, water, barren, and live oak. The white, turkey, and chesnut are used for ship-timber; the acorn of the latter very superiour in size to any other. Red oak is chiefly used for pipe-staves, and exported to most parts of Europe, and the West Indies. Black oak is a dry wood, and easily splits; is chiefly used for the rails and fences of their enclosures. Ground oak is bushy, and seldom exceeds six feet in height; it bears a small acorn of a very superiour flavour, which is the chief food of the deer, and sheep, who run wild in the woods. Water and barren oak are small and bushy, and only used for firing. Live oak is *said* to be very superiour to all the rest, and the best *ship-timber* in the world. I am informed it is a sort of evergreen, seldom met with north of the Carolinas.

Oct. 26th. —Went to Philadelphia. —After crossing the Delaware, I found the land very different from the Jersey shore; a fine stiff black soil, the clover growing spontaneously. The city exhibited a most melancholy spectacle; most of the houses and stores shut up, and grass growing in many of the streets; what few *white* inhabitants I met with had a most dejected appearance. The disorder has been most favourable to the softer sex; women with child, and those above and under a certain age, were in general free from the infection: but so fatal has it proved to the other sex, that, in Apple-tree-alley, which does not exceed fifty yards in length, there are upwards of sixty widows within these two months. The total loss on this melancholy occasion already exceeds four thousand, nearly one tenth of the inhabitants! Returning to Woodbury, I met with a quaker, who informed me of the *cause* of the infectious disorder in the Great City: "*It is* a judgment on the inhabitants for their sins, insomuch that they sent to England for a number of play-actors, singers, and *musicians*, who were *actually arrived*; and as a just judgment on the Philadelphians for encouraging these *children of iniquity*, they were now afflicted with the yellow fever. " I told him, that more likely the sins of the *quakers* had drawn down this judgment on the city *of brotherly love,* and that it was now scourged for *their* hypocrisy, lying, canting, and other *manifold iniquities.*

Oct. 27th. —Very cold wind at N. W. In the evening snow.

Oct. 29th. —Favourable accounts from Philadelphia: the late cold weather has entirely stopped the progress of the disorder.

November 26th.

Set out for Annapolis, and arrived there in health, the 29th, at five in the afternoon.

Annapolis, 17th December, 1793.

DEAR FRIEND,

The bay of Chesapeak is one of the largest in the world. From it's entrance, between capes Henry and Charles, to the mouth of the Susquana, which forms the head of the bay, the distance is two hundred and eighty miles, through which great extent of water the tide ebbs and flows. This bay receives into it's bosom the following rivers; viz. the Patomac, the Rappahanock, the Patapsico, the York, the James, the Severn, and the Elk, beside innumerable creeks, and small streams. On an inlet from this bay, about two hundred miles from it's entrance from the Atlantic, stands Annapolis, the capital of the state of Maryland, so called in honour of queen Anne, as appears from the following extract from their charter: —

"Anne, by the grace of God, queen of Great Britain, &c....

"To all, and singular, our faithful subjects within our province of Maryland, greeting.... Whereas there is a pleasant and commodious place for trade... laid out for a town, and port, and called Annapolis, in honour of us. "

This city was intended for the emporium of the province; and surely no spot ever *seemed* better calculated for a town of trade and commerce. Far to the south, and in one of the most pleasant and healthy situations in America; as the seat of government, being the greatest, and indeed then *only* mercantile town in the province; the bay of Chesapeak, and adjacent rivers, wafting the tobacco and other produce of the country to this mart at a trifling expense; a harbour where ships might ride at anchor in perfect security, and where wharfs, with sufficient depth of water for a vessel of eight hundred tons, might be formed with very little trouble: but unfortunately these advantages were rendered abortive by the bite of a small insect; the worms are so troublesome in these waters, that a vessel lying in this harbour during the summer months will be as full of holes as a honey-comb. Baltimore, a town on a similar inlet from the bay, about thirty miles hence, being free from this plague, (by having a great proportion of fresh water from the Patapsico in it's harbour) has drawn all the trade from the *capital*: the Annapolians have now but *one* square-rigged vessel belonging to their port, while their rivals have many hundreds, and drive a brisk trade to the four quarters of the globe.

Annapolis is whimsically laid out, the streets verging from each other, like rays from a centre. It is still the seat of government; and it's state-house is by much the best building I have seen in America. This little city is now the retreat of some of the best families in the state. The inhabitants in general are passionately fond of theatrical entertainments, and received us with a degree of kindness and hospitality which claims our warmest acknowledgments. I spend my time here very agreeably. The politeness, ease, and conviviality of the Annapolians form a strong and pleasing contrast to the behaviour of the stiff, gloomy and unsocial bigots I was lately surrounded with in the Jerseys. Next to Virginia, this state was the most famous for tobacco-plantations; but the people now find the culture of wheat more profitable, as well as less injurious to the soil. No plant impoverishes the earth so much by it's growth as tobacco; many plantations, owing to successive crops of this *weed*, are what is here called *worn out*; formerly, when their land was in this state, instead of endeavouring to bring it round by a few fallow years and manure, as in England, they immediately cleared a fresh tract. They now begin to use manure, and have discovered a very extraordinary kind; viz. antediluvian oyster-shells, large beds of which are found a few feet beneath the surface of the earth in several parts of the state[Footnote: See Bartram's Account of a similar Bed in Georgia, page 213.]: these being laid on the land, are, by the effect of the air, crumbled into dust in a few days, and fertilize the earth in an astonishing degree. —Farewell. —Conclude me

Yours very sincerely, &c.

Philadelphia, 27th February, 1794.

DEAR FRIEND,

On the fourth instant I left Annapolis on my way to this city. After travelling eight miles, we passed through a long and dreary wood; here we met two negroes conveying a coffin on a sort of sledge. On inquiry, one of them informed us, the coffin contained the corpse of his mother; that on the death of his old master, his parents were sold to different planters, which his father took so much to heart, that he died soon after; his mother only survived him about five months; and they were now complying with her last request, which was, to be carried to a plantation about eight miles thence, and there buried with her husband. There seemed a great degree of dejection in the poor fellow's countenance; and I could not help telling him, by way of consolation, that his father and mother were gone to a better place, where there was no distinction of colour, and where no white man would dare again to part them; but as *words* are *wind*, we agreed to administer some more *solid* consolation, which the black man received with a look of gratitude, then cast his eye towards his mother's corpse, and shed a silent tear. Why was not *Sterne* present at this scene?

I slept at an inn, about twenty miles from Annapolis, where we supped in the American fashion on fried squirrels and coffee, the former excellent.

Feb. 5th. —Arrived at Baltimore, and hired a caravan with four horses, which is here called a stage: the same afternoon we arrived at the Susquana. This noble river, which is here about a mile and a quarter wide, was frozen hard. Our *advanced guard* crossed the day before, in a ferry boat: this circumstance will give you some idea of the severity of the cold in this climate. A negro slave, belonging to the ferry, undertook to drive our stage over the river for two dollars, which his *master put into his pocket*, and ordered *Sambo* to proceed; the fellow drove boldly, and was across in a few minutes, the ice cracking most horribly all the way. I suppose I need not inform you, we were *not* in the carriage.

On the evening of the 7th we slept at Wilmington, a pleasantly situate town on the banks of a creek, which joins the Delaware, about thirty miles below Philadelphia. There are about thirty square-rigged vessels, beside sloops, and schooners, belonging to this port, which was originally a danish settlement.

The next morning I walked to Brandywine, to see the grist mills, which are said to be the best in the United States. About five miles from this village was fought the battle of Brandywine. This was Washington's last effort to stop general Howe's progress, and save Philadelphia. The royal army being victorious, they got possession of that city without opposition. General Washington, after rallying his troops, took a very advantageous situation on a chain of hills, a few miles west of the British army.

We dined at Chester. This little town is situated on the Delaware, and is the same to Philadelphia that Gravesend is to London. Ships outward bound here receive their passengers, &c. &c.

At four the same day, arrived in this city, distant from Annapolis one hundred and forty one miles, and from Baltimore one hundred and eleven. Farewell.

Yours, &c.

Philadelphia, March 1st, 1794.

DEAR SIR,

I perfectly agree with you, that the form of government in a great measure *affects*, or rather *forms* the manners, and way of thinking of the people; but must decline answering the queries in your last, at least for the present. I have not been long enough in these states to draw any fair conclusions on these subjects; but that you may not be wholly disappointed, I send you two anecdotes, on which you may depend.

Peter Brown, a blacksmith of this city, having made his fortune, set up his coach; but so far from being ashamed of the means by which he acquired his riches, he caused a large *anvil* to be painted on each pannel of his carriage, with two naked arms in the act of striking. The motto, *"By this I got ye. "*

Benjamin Whitall, high sheriff for the county of Gloster, West Jersey, being obliged soon after his appointment to attend an execution, not approving of Jack Ketch's clumsy method of *finishing the law*, fairly tucked up the next criminal *himself*. Such behaviour in Germany would have branded him with eternal infamy, but is in this country (I think justly) thought a spirited action of a man, who was above receiving the emoluments of an office, without performing the most essential duty annexed to it himself.

I have often heard it asserted, that a servant should be born under an absolute monarchy: whether this observation is just or not, I cannot tell, but I know, that a republic is *not* the place to find good servants. If you want to hire a maid servant in this city, she will not allow you the title of *master*, or herself to be called a *servant*; and you may think yourself favoured if she condescends to inform you when she means to spend an evening abroad; if you grumble at all this, she will leave you at a moment's warning; after which you will find it very difficult to procure another on any terms. This is one of the natural consequences of liberty and equality.

Farewell, &c.

March 3d, 1794.

Dear friend,

Philadelphia, the present seat of government, both of the state of Pensylvania, and of the whole federal union, consisted, in the year 1681, of half a dozen miserable huts, inhabited by a few emigrants from Sweden; when the celebrated William Penn obtained a charter from king Charles the Second, for a certain tract of unsettled country in North America, extending from twelve miles north of Newcastle, along the courses of the Delaware, and a meridian line from its head, to the 43d degree of north latitude, and westward, 5 degrees of longitude from its eastern bounds.

In the year following, he arrived, and in 1701 the city was finally laid out from Cedar-street to Vine-street, forming an oblong square of two miles in length, from the river Delaware to the Scuylkill; and about a mile in width. It was the wish of the founder, that the fronts facing the *two* rivers should be *equally* built upon; by which means the city would naturally meet in the centre; but they have not only deviated from the original plan, by running the city along the banks of the Delaware, *beyond* the aforesaid streets, which formed the bounds in that direction, but have left the *Scuylkill* front without a single street.

Philadelphia is situate in latitude 39 deg. 56 min. north, and long. 75 deg. 8 min. west from Greenwich, on a narrow neck of land, between the rivers Delaware and Scuylkill, on the Pensylvania banks of the latter, where this river is about one mile wide, and one hundred and twenty (following it's course) from the Atlantic Ocean. This noble river affords a safe navigation for vessels of a thousand tuns burden up to the wharfs of the city. The Scuylkill (though by no means so wide) has nearly the same depth of water.

Philadelphia is the first port in the Union. The total value of it's exports in the year 1793, was 695736 dollars; the total of flower shipped in the year 1792 was 420000 barrels, and in the spring only of 1793 it exceeded 200000 barrels.

The total of inward entries at Philadelphia, in 1793, was 1414 vessels of different sizes, of which 477 were ships or brigs.

It is foreign from the subject of this city, but I cannot help informing you, that the imports of the *United States* from *Great Britain* alone, in the year 1791, were stated at 19502070 dollars, (chiefly of *manufactured articles*) and have been considerably increasing every year since.

By a slight inspection of the plan, you will perceive the great regularity observed in laying out this city; the streets intersect each other at right angles, the centre street, north and south, is 113 feet wide; that east and west 100 feet; and the other principal streets 50 feet wide. Had equal care been taken to build the houses uniformly, and their height in proportion to the width of the streets, this city would have been uncommonly beautiful; but except that the fronts of the buildings were not permitted to extend beyond the line laid down in the plan, every man built his house (to use the language of the first settlers,) "as it seemed good in his own eyes. "

The first object of an industrious emigrant, who means to settle in Philadelphia, is to purchase a lot of ground in one of the vacant streets. He erects a small building forty or fifty feet from the line laid out for him by the city surveyor, and lives there till he can afford to build a house; when his former habitation serves him for a kitchen and wash-house. I have observed buildings in this state in the heart of the city; but they are more common in the outskirts. Our friend Wright is exactly in this situation; but I am afraid it will be many years before he will be able to build in *front*.

The buildings in this city are about two thirds of brick, and the rest of wood. The foundations of the former are in general of a species of marble; the bricks are uncommonly well manufactured; and these buildings are more firmly constructed than in Europe. Those of wood are the reverse, which you will easily credit, when I inform you, that when a house of this description is offered for sale, it is by no means understood, as in England, that the *land* on which it stands is included in the purchase. They have a method of removing these buildings *entire*. A house *travelling* in this manner through the streets of the city is to a European a truly grotesque and extraordinary sight.

During the time the British troops had possession of this city in the last war, they were much distressed for fuel, and obliged to cut down all the wood they could meet with; upwards of a thousand acres of peach and apple orchard were destroyed, belonging to one family. This destruction of the trees has materially hurt the prospects for three or four miles on the Pensylvania side; the opposite Jersey shore (except the plantations) is one entire forest.

Philadelphia is at present supplied with water from pumps, placed in different parts of the city; but a company of adventurers are bringing water from above the falls of Scuylkill, in the manner of the New River in London: but mean to improve on sir Hugh Middleton's plan, by making their aqueduct also serve the purposes of inland navigation.

The inhabitants are in general very fond of theatrical representations; their new theatre is an elegant building, from a design the subscribers obtained from London, where the principal scenes were painted by Richardson and Rooker. The receipts of the house have exceeded one thousand six hundred dollars.

The fair Philadelphians are by no means so fond of walking, as the English ladies; not that they have any *great dislike* to a *trip* into the *country*, but it is not fashionable even for a maid servant to make use of her *legs* on these occasions; the consequence is, that there are 806 two and four wheeled machines entered at the office, and pay duty, as *pleasure carriages*, most of which are for hire; and yet the inhabitants do not exceed 50000, of whom there are not three individuals but follow some profession, trade, or employment. In a few days I shall have an opportunity of sending you a publication, which will give you a more ample account of this city than you now receive from

Yours, &c.

Since writing this letter, the seat of government of the state has been removed to Lancaster, as being nearer the centre; for the same reason, that of the general government of the United States, will, in the year 1800, be removed to the federal city, now building in the district of Columbia.

Several *uniform* and elegant rows of houses have *lately* been built.

Philadelphia, March 7th, 1794.

DEAR SIR,

It is a general observation with respect to the English, that they eat more animal food than the people of any other nation. The following statement of the manner of living of the Americans[Footnote: By the term *American* you must understand a white man descended from a native of the Old Continent; and by the term *Indian*, or *Savage*, one of the aborigines of the New World.] will convince you of the falsity of this opinion.

About eight or nine in the morning they breakfast on tea and coffee, attended always with what they call *relishes*, such as salt fish, beef-steaks, sausages, broiled-fowls, ham, bacon, &c. At two they dine on what is usual in England, with a variety of american dishes, such as bear, opossum, racoon, &c. At six or seven in the evening they have their supper, which is exactly the same as their breakfast, with the addition of what cold meat is left at dinner. I have often wondered how they acquired this method of living, which is by no means calculated for the climate; such stimulating food at breakfast and supper naturally causes thirst, and there being no other beverage at these meals than tea, or coffee, they are apt to drink too freely of them, particularly the female part of the family; which, during the excessive heats in summer, is relaxing and debilitating; and in winter, by opening the pores, exposes them to colds of the most dangerous kind.

The manner of living I have been describing is that of people in moderate circumstances; but this taste for *relishes* with coffee and tea extends to all ranks of people in these states. Soon after my arrival at this city, I went on a party of pleasure to a sort of tea-garden and *tavern*[Footnote: By the word *tavern*, in America, is meant an inn or public house of any description.], romantically situate on the bank of the Scuylkill. At six in the evening we ordered coffee, which I was informed they were here famous for serving *in style*. I took a memorandum of what was on the table; viz. *coffee, cheese, sweet cakes, hung beef, sugar, pickled salmon, butter, crackers, ham, cream,* and *bread.* The ladies all declared, it was a most *charming relish*!

Yours sincerely, &c.

Philadelphia, March 12th, 1794.

Dear Friend,

The price of labour in this country is very great, owing to the prospect an industrious man has of procuring an independance by cultivating a tract of the waste lands; many millions of acres of which are how on sale by government; to say nothing of those held by individuals. The money arising from the sale of the former is appropriated to the discharge of the national debt.

During my residence in Jersey, I was at no little pains to inform myself of the difficulties attending a back settler. We will suppose a person making such an attempt to possess one hundred pounds, though many have been successful with a much less sum: his first care is to purchase about three hundred acres of land, which, if it is in a remote western settlement, he will procure for about nineteen pounds sterling: he may know the quality of the land by the trees, with which it is entirely covered. The hickory and the walnut are an infallible sign of a rich, and every species of fir, of a barren, sandy, and unprofitable soil. When his land is properly registered, his next care is to provide himself with a horse, a plough, and other implements of agriculture; a rifle, a fowling piece, some ammunition, and a large dog of the blood-hound breed, to hunt deer. We will suppose him arrived at the place of his destination in spring, as soon as the ground is clear of frost. No sooner is the arrival of a new settler circulated, than, for many miles round, his neighbours flock to him: they all assist in erecting his hut; this is done with logs; a bricklayer is only wanting to make his chimney and oven. He then clears a few acres by cutting down the large trees about four feet from the *ground*[Footnote: These stumps are many years rotting, and, when completely rotted, afford an excellent manure.], grubs up the underwood, splits some of the large timber for railing fences, and sets fire to the rest upon the spot; ploughs round the stumps of the large timber, and in May plants maize, or indian corn. In October he has a harvest of eight hundred or a thousand fold. This is every thing to him and his family. Indian corn, ground and made into cakes, answers the end of bread, and when boiled with meat, and a small proportion of a sort of kidney-bean (which it is usual to sow with this grain), it makes an excellent dish, which they call *hominy*. They also coarsely pound the indian corn, and boil it for five hours; this is by the Indians called *mush*; and, when a proportion of milk is added, forms their breakfast. Indian corn is also the best food for horses employed in agriculture in this climate: black cattle, deer, and hogs are very fond of it, and fatten better than on any other grain. It is also excellent food for turkies, and other poultry.

When this harvest is in, he provides himself with a cow, and a few sheep and hogs; the latter run wild in the woods. But for a few years he depends chiefly on his *rifle*, and *faithful dog*; with these he provides his family with deer, bear, racoon, &c. ; but what he values most are the black, and gray squirrels; these animals are large and numerous, are excellent roasted, and make a soup exceedingly rich and nourishing.

He gradually clears his land, a few acres every year, and begins to plant wheat, tobacco, &c. These, together with what hogs, and other increase of his stock he can spare, as also the skins of deer, bear, and other animals he shoots in the woods, he exchanges with the nearest storekeeper, for clothing, sugar, coffee, &c.

In this state he suffers much for want of the comforts and even *necessaries* of life. Suppose him afflicted with a flux or fever, attacked by a panther, bitten by a rattle-snake, or any other of the dreadful circumstances peculiar to his situation: but, above all, suppose a war to break out between the Indians, and him, and his whole family scalped, and their plantations burnt!

The following extract from an American work very feelingly describes him under these cruel apprehensions: —

EXTRACT.

"You know the position of our settlement; therefore I need not describe it. To the west it is enclosed by a chain of mountains, reaching to——. To the east, the country is yet but very thinly inhabited. We are almost insulated, and the houses are at a considerable distance from each other. From the mountains we have but too much reason to expect our dreadful enemy, the Indians; and the wilderness is a harbour, where it is impossible to find them. It is a door through which they can enter our country at any time; and as they seem determined to destroy the whole frontier, our fate cannot be far distant. From lake Champlain almost all has been conflagrated, one after another. What renders these incursions still more dreadful is, that they most commonly take place in the dead of the night. We never go to our fields, but we are seized with an involuntary fear, which lessens our strength, and weakens our labour. No other subject of discourse intervenes between the different accounts, which spread through the country, of successive acts of devastation; and these, told in chimney corners, swell themselves in our affrighted imaginations into the most terrific ideas. We never sit down, either to dinner, or supper, but the least noise spreads a general alarm, and prevents us from enjoying the comforts of our meals. The very appetite proceeding from labour and peace of mind is gone! Our sleep is disturbed by the most frightful dreams! Sometimes I start awake, as if the great hour of danger was come; at other times the howling of our dogs seems to announce the arrival of the enemy: we leap out of bed, and run to arms; my poor wife, with panting bosom, and silent tears, takes leave of me, as if we were to see each other no more. She snatches the youngest children from their beds, who, suddenly awakened, increase by their innocent questions the horrour of the dreadful moment! She tries to hide them in the cellar, as if our cellar was inaccessible to the fire! I place all my servants at the window, and myself at the door, where I am determined to perish. Fear industriously increases every sound; we all listen; each communicates to each other his fears and conjectures. We remain thus, sometimes for whole hours, our hearts and our minds racked by the most anxious suspense! What a dreadful situation! A thousand times worse than that of a soldier engaged in the midst of a most severe conflict! Sometimes feeling the spontaneous courage of a man, I seem to wish for the decisive minute; the next instant a message from my wife, sent by one of the children, quite unmans me. Away goes my courage, and I descend again into the deepest despondency: at last, finding it was a false alarm, we return once more to our beds; but what good can the sleep of nature do us, when interrupted with *such* scenes? "

* * * * *

But we will suppose our planter to have escaped the scalping knife and tomahawk; and in the course of years situate in a thick, settled neighbourhood of planters like himself, who have struggled through all the foregoing difficulties: he is now a man of some consequence, builds a house by the side of his former hut, which now serves him for a kitchen; and as he is comfortably situate, we will leave him to the enjoyment of the fruits of his industry.

Such a being has often ideas of liberty, and a contempt of vassalage and slavery, which do honour to human nature.

The planter I have endeavoured to describe, I have supposed to be sober and industrious: but when a man of an opposite description makes such an attempt, he often degenerates into a demisavage; he cultivates no more land than will barely supply the family with bread, or rather makes his wife, and children perform that office. His whole employment is to procure skins, and furs, to exchange for rum, brandy, and ammunition; for this purpose he is often for several days together in the woods, without seeing a human being. He is by no means at a loss; his rifle supplies him with food, and at night he cuts down some boughs with his tomahawk, and constructs a *wigwam*[Footnote: The Indian name for their huts so constructed.], in which he spends the night, stretched on the skins of those animals he has killed in the course of his excursion. This manner of living he learned from his savage neighbours, the Indians, and like them calls every other state of life *slavery*. It sometimes happens, that an unsuccessful back settler joins the Indians at war with the states. When this is the case, it is observed he is, if possible, more cruel than his new allies; he eagerly imbibes all the vices of the savages, without a single spark of their virtues. Farewell,

Yours &c.

Philadelphia, March 18th, 1794.

Dear Friend,

My present intention is to give you some conception of the family of a planter, whose ancestors had in some degree gone through all the difficulties I described in my last.

We will suppose them descended from the original english emigrants, who came over with Penn; like them, to possess a high sense of religion; and that this family are now in the quiet possession of about three hundred acres of land, their own *property*[Footnote: There are very few *farms* properly so called in the United States.], situate in Pennsylvania, about seventy or eighty miles from Philadelphia. Whatever difficulties they, or their ancestors, struggled formerly with, are now over; their lands are cleared, and in the bosom of a fine country, with a sure market for every article of produce they can possibly raise, and entirely out of the reach of the most desperate predatory excursions of the savages.

They enjoy a happy state of mediocrity[Footnote: The quakers in particular. I have seen at a meeting in West Jersey, in a very small town, upwards of two hundred carriages, one horse chairs, and light waggons, which are machines peculiar to this country, and well adapted to the sandy soil of the state of New Jersey; they are covered like a caravan, and will hold eight persons; the benches are removable at pleasure, and they are also used to convey the produce of the country to market.], between riches and poverty, perhaps the most enviable of all situations. When the boys of this family are numerous, those the father cannot provide for at home, and who prefer a planter's life to a trade, or profession, are, when married, presented with two or three hundred acres of uncultivated land, which their parents purchase for them as near home as possible. The young couple are supplied with stock, and supported till they have a sufficient quantity of land cleared to provide for themselves.

If unsuccessful through want of industry, &c., they often sell off, and emigrate to Kentucky, or some other new country seven or eight hundred miles to the S. W., and begin the world again as back settlers.

The daughters are brought up in habits of virtue and industry; the strict notions of female delicacy, instilled into their minds from their earliest infancy, never entirely forsake them. Even when one of these girls is decoyed from the peaceful dwelling of her parents, and left by her infamous seducer a prey to poverty and prostitution in a *brothel* at Philadelphia, her whole appearance is neat, and breathes an air of modesty: you see nothing in her dress, language, or behaviour, that could give you any reason to guess at her unfortunate situation; (how unlike her unhappy sisters so circumstanced in England!) she by no means gives over the idea of a husband, she is seldom disappointed: and, I am informed, often makes an excellent wife.

The chief amusement of the country girls in winter is sleighing, of which they are passionately fond, as indeed are the whole sex in this country. I never heard a woman speak of this diversion but with rapture. You have doubtless read a description of a *sleigh*, or sledge, as it is common in all northern countries, and can only be used on the snow. In British America this amusement may be followed nearly all the winter; but so far to the south as Pennsylvania, the snow seldom lies on the ground more than seven or eight days together. The consequence is, that every moment that will admit of sleighing is seized on with avidity. The tavern and inn-keepers are up all night; and the whole country is in motion. When the snow begins to fall, our planter's daughters provide hot sand, which at night they place in bags at the bottom of the sleigh. Their sweethearts attend with a couple of horses, and away they glide with astonishing velocity; visiting their friends for many miles round the country. But in large towns, in order to have a sleighing frolic in *style*, it is necessary to provide a *fiddler* who is placed at the head of the sleigh, and plays all the way. At every inn they meet with on the road, the company alight and have a dance. But I perceive I am *dancing* from my subject, which I suppose you are by this time heartily tired of; I shall therefore conclude, by assuring you,

I am

Yours sincerely, &c.

"There be also store of frogs, which in the spring time will chirp, and whistle like birds: there be also toads, that will creep to the top of trees, and sit there croaking, to the wonderment of strangers! "

"To a stranger walking for the first time in these woods during the summer, this appears the land of enchantment: he hears a thousand noises, without being able to discern from whence or from what animal they proceed, but which are, in fact, the discordant notes of five different species of frogs! "

Philadelphia, April 27th, 1794.

DEAR FRIEND,

Previous to my coming to this country, I recollect reading the foregoing passages, the first in a history of New England, published in London, in the year 1671; and the other in a similar production of a later date.

Prepared as I was to hear something extraordinary from these animals, I confess the first frog *concert* I heard in America was so much beyond any thing I could conceive of the *powers* of these *musicians*, that I was truly astonished. This *performance* was *al fresco*, and took place on the night of the 18th instant, in a large *swamp*, where there were at least ten thousand *performers*; and I really believe not two *exactly* in the same pitch, if the octave can possibly admit of so many divisions or shades of semitones. An hibernian musician, who, like myself, was present for the first time at this *concert* of *antimusic*, exclaimed, "By Jasus but they stop out of tune to a *nicety!* "

I have been since informed by an *amateur*, who resided many years in this country, and made this species of *music* his peculiar study, that on these occasions the *treble* is performed by the tree-frogs, the smallest and most *beautiful* species; they are always of the same colour as the bark of the tree they inhabit, and their note is not unlike the chirp of a cricket: the next in size are our *counter tenors*; they have a note resembling the *setting* of a *saw*. A still larger species sing *tenor*; and the *under part* is supported by the bull-frogs; which are as large as a man's foot, and *bellow* out the *bass* in a tone as loud and sonorous as that of the animal from which they take their name.

To an Englishman lately arrived in this country there are other phenomena, equally curious; as *fire-flies, night-hawks &c. ;* but, above all, such tremendous peals of thunder and flashes of lightning, as can be conceived only by those who have been in southern latitudes.

I have often thought, if an enthusiastic *cockney*, of weak nerves, who had never been out of the sound of Bow bell, could suddenly be conveyed from his bed, in the middle of the night, and laid, fast asleep, in an american swamp, he would, on waking, fancy himself in the infernal regions: his first sensation would be from the stings of a myriad of mosquitoes; waking with the smart, his ears would be assailed with the horrid noises of the frogs; on lifting up his eyes he would have a faint view of the night-hawks, flapping their ominous wings over his devoted head, visible only from the glimmering light of the fire-flies, which he would naturally conclude were sparks from the bottomless pit. Nothing would be wanting at this moment to complete the illusion, but one of those dreadful explosions of thunder and lightning, so *extravagantly* described by Lee, in Oedipus:—

"Call you these peals of thunder, but the yawn or bellowing clouds? by Jove, they seem to me the world's last groans, and those large sheets of flame it's last blaze! "

I have often traversed the woods by myself at night, and sometimes during *such scenes*; and though I was conscious that all round me proceeded from natural causes, I could not at these times entirely forget,

"All that the *priest* and all the nurse had taught. "

Farewell. —Believe me

Yours very sincerely, &c.,

Philadelphia, August 10th, 1794.

DEAR SIR,

Having a few weeks vacation at the theatre, we agreed upon a scheme to give three concerts at Lancaster, a town in Pennsylvania, about seventy miles west of this city. Our band was small, but select; and our singers Darley, and miss Broadhurst. We crossed the Scuylkill about two miles below the Falls.

The country, which, from the Atlantic to this spot, is nearly a level, now abruptly swells into hills, and rises as you advance westerly, till you reach the Allegany mountains, the great *back bone* of America, as the Indians call that chain of mountains. There is then a considerable descent; but that the country rises afterward for many hundred miles is certain from the course of the rivers. No traveller has penetrated so far west, in these latitudes, as to find a river which did not ultimately run into the Atlantic Ocean,

We slept about a mile from the *Pioli*. I took a walk to reconnoitre the field of battle, with one who was present at that horrid affair.

General Wayne was here completely surprised, but had his revenge at Stoney Point.

After St. Claire's defeat, he was appointed by Congress to the command of the continental army in the present indian war. The fatal surprise at the Pioli has been an excellent lesson for him; since his present appointment he has established the most rigid discipline: this is of the utmost consequence in any army; but particularly so in *that* he commands, as they have to contend with the most subtle and desperate foe on earth, flushed with their late victory over St. Claire. —In a former indian war, an army lay with it's rear and flanks well secured; a river three quarters of a mile broad in its front, and no enemy within fifty miles. A body of Indians, being informed by their scouts of the situation of this army, made a forced march, crossed the river in the night, on rafts hastily constructed, completely surprised the camp before sun-rise in the morning, butchered all before them, and made their retreat good with their scalps and plunder, before the enemy recovered from the general consternation. The system of military tactics Wayne has introduced is admirably adapted to the perilous service, in which he is engaged. He fights the Indians in their own way, and scalps are now taken on both sides. —There is expected to be warm work this campaign; and it is generally imagined Wayne will meet with the fate of Braddock and St. Clare. A few military men I have discoursed with, are of another opinion; they tell me the rifle-men of the western army were recruited from Kentucky, and other remote settlements, and are all experienced *back-woods-men*, who have been great part of their lives in the habits of Indian fighting; that the general is forming a body of cavalry, on principles entirely new, from which much is expected; in short, that Wayne will oblige the Indians to *bury the hatchet* on his own terms. The Indian war is not popular. It has met with much opposition both in the General Assemblies of the States, and in Congress.

The devastation that has (even within the present century) taken place among the brave and independent aborigines of this continent, is really shocking to humanity[Footnote: The Cherokees are by no means the formidable body of warriors they were 40 years ago. The original possessors of the vast tract of land which forms North Carolina, are reduced to a single family; and several tribes of the eastern Indians actually exterminated.].

I spent the evening at the Pioli, with a surgeon of the american army lately from the scene of action; he gave me a disgusting account of the misunderstanding that subsists between the american citizens on the frontiers, and their neighbours in Upper Canada. It seems the Canadians are accused of assisting the indians in the decisive action against St. Clare.

As many of the descendants of the original french settlers have indian blood in their veins, the charge is not improbable, as far as relates to a few *individuals*, but that they received either the connivance, or protection of *government*, (as the Americans assert) is totally without foundation.

I never take up a western newspaper that does not teem with the most illiberal abuse of the british government. It would therefore be impossible to exonerate certain american citizens from *their share of provocation*, and a wish to blow up the hardly-extinguished embers of the late war. This temper is kept alive by french agents, who use every means of inflaming the public mind, by the most flagrant exaggerations of the late captures, &c. : and so successful have they been in their misrepresentations, that a war with England would at this time be very popular.

Aug. 30th. —You can conceive nothing more beautifully romantic, than the appearance of the country during the latter part of this day's journey. The hills, bold, rounding, and lofty, are covered with wood to their very summit. In the midst of this wild scenery is the mighty *Susquana*, above a mile wide, dashing over rocks and precipices, seventy or eighty miles distant from the flow of the tide. A similar body of running water, perfectly clear and transparent, with so many hundred cascades as beautify the Susquana, is perhaps no where else to be met with. Unfortunately these very beauties render the navigation of this noble river impracticable.

Aug. 31st. —Arrived at Lancaster, a prettily situate town, of about nine hundred houses. It is reckoned the largest inland town south of New England, and indeed the only large town without some kind of navigation; to remedy this inconvenience as much as possible, a turnpike road (very superiour to any thing of the kind in America, and which will cost three thousand dollars per mile,) is forming from Philadelphia, through Lancaster, to the Susquana. I before told you this river, owing to the rocks and falls, was not navigable; but I forgot to inform you, that the inhabitants of the back country contrive to waft the produce of their plantations down the river on floats, during the floods, in spring and fall; which will be conveyed by means of this new road to Philadelphia, whence it will be exported to the west indian or european markets.

The only manufactory in Lancaster is one of rifles; they have contracted to supply the continental army with these *"mortal engines."*

I have heard a hundred improbable stories relative to what was done with the rifle by famous marksmen in America, such as shooting an apple from a child's head, &c; to which I could not give credit: but, I have no reason to doubt the following feat: as it was actually performed before many hundred inhabitants of this borough, and the adjacent country. —During the late war, in the year 1775, a company of riflemen, formed from the back woodsmen of Virginia, were quartered here for some time: two of them *alternately* held a board only nine inches square between his knees, while his comrade fired a ball through it from a distance of one hundred paces! The board is still preserved; and I am assured by several who were present, that it was performed without any manner of deception.

Lancaster was originally a german settlement; the inhabitants were so desirous of perpetuating their language, that they established german schools for the education of the rising generation; but their descendants, finding the inconvenience of being without a knowledge of English, now send their children first to the german, and afterward to the english schools; by which means they acquire a tolerable idea of both languages. They still retain many characteristics of their ancestors; such as frugality, plainness in dress, &c. At our first concert, three clownish-looking fellows came into the room, and, after sitting a few minutes, (the weather being *warm*, not to say *hot*) very composedly took off their coats: they were in the usual summer dress of farmers servants in this part of the country; that is to say, *without* either stockings or breeches, a loose pair of trowsers being the only succedaneum. As we fixed our admission at a dollar each, (here seven shillings and sixpence,) we expected this circumstance would be sufficient to exclude *such* characters; but on inquiry, I found (to my very great surprise!) our three *sans culottes* were german *gentlemen* of considerable property in the neighbourhood!

They manage these matters better at Hanover; (a settlement of germans about forty miles hence.) One of the articles of their dancing assembly is in these words; "No gentleman to enter the ball-room without *breeches*, or to be allowed to dance without his *coat.* "

All the back parts of Pennsylvania were in general cleared, and settled by german, and irish emigrants; but the former are commonly more prosperous than their neighbours, whom they excel in sobriety and economy, and have also a much better understanding amongst themselves.

An irish family often arrives, and purchases a plantation; which for some years brings them good crops, but for want of manure will in time be worn out (a very common case in America.) When in this situation they offer it for sale, the adjacent german families club a sum of money, purchase the land, plough it well, and let it remain in this state for three or four years: they then place an emigrant family from their *own country* upon the farm, who, by indefatigable industry and manure, soon bring the land round, pay for the estate by installments, and live very comfortably. Some of the best plantations in Pennsylvania were originally left in this manner. The irish family go two or three hundred miles up the country, where they can purchase as much land as they please, from sixpence to a dollar per acre: here they literally *break fresh ground*, and begin the world again. To some timorous people, their new situation would be thought dangerous, as they are liable to a visit from the Indians, and perishing by the scalping knife and tomahawk. —See a former letter on back settlers.

Aug. 6th. —We returned to Philadelphia, not *overloaded* with *cash*, but with more than was sufficient for our expenses, which, owing to several excursions from Lancaster, were not trifling. —Farewel. — Believe me

Yours very sincerely.

Philadelphia, 14th August, 1794.

DEAR SIR,

By captain H——, of the Betsy, who will deliver this letter, I have sent you specimens of the federal coinage.

When that government was formed, a mint was established, and a coinage issued on a new plan. This was much wanted, as scarcely three of the states agreed as to the value currency of a dollar. Here it was seven shillings and sixpence, in South Carolina four shillings and eight pence, at New York eight shillings, and in the New England states six shillings. According to the new regulations, all *nominal* coins are exploded, and the silver dollar, weighing 17 dwts. 6 grs. [Footnote: This is the exact weight of the spanish milled dollar, which, as well as the divisions, are allowed to pass current; they consist of the half, quarter, eighth, and sixteenth, also the pistreen, or fifth, and the half pistreen, or tenth.], is fixed as the standard, divided into one hundred decimal parts; these are of copper, and called cents. All taxes, duties and imposts, that extend to the *whole Union*, are levied in these coins *only*. The other federal coins, like the english guineas and crowns, never appear on the public accounts.

Those of *gold* are eagles, half eagles, and quarter eagles, value ten, five, and two and a half, dollars: of *silver*, the half, quarter, tenth, and twentieth of the standard dollar; or fifty, twenty-five, ten, and five cents: of *copper*, the half cent, or two hundredth part of a dollar. The principle on which this coinage is formed is so very simple, that the proportion they bear to each other, and the standard dollar may be found with the utmost facility. Indeed little else is wanted than the adding or cutting off figures or ciphers: for instance, the public accounts being kept in two columns, dollars, and cents; suppose in adding up the latter, you find they amount to 27621, you have only to cut off the two right hand figures, and their value stands thus; 276 dollars, 21 cents. To reduce eagles to dollars, add a cipher, and vice versa. To reduce half, and quarter eagles to dollars, you have only to divide by 2 or 4 previous to adding the cipher.

But though the federal government has succeeded in establishing it's coinage, the *people* cannot be persuaded (the wholesale merchants, and a few enlightened citizens excepted,) to come into this scheme; *they* obstinately insist on buying, selling, and keeping their accounts in the *good old way of their fathers!* that is to say, in *currency*, by pounds, shillings, and pence; and nothing can be more complex, as they have not a single *coin* in circulation of the *real* or *nominal* value of any of them. If you are to pay the sum of three shillings and fourpence halfpenny, (without having recourse to the federal scheme) you must provide yourself with three silver divisions of the Spanish dollar, viz. the fourth, eighth, and sixteenth, three english halfpence, two of George the Second, and one of his present majesty[Footnote: Owing to the quantity of counterfeit english halfpence of the present reign now in circulation in these states, those of king George the Third, whether counterfeit or not, are depreciated to the 360th part of a dollar.]; the nominal value of which, added together, make that sum within a very trifling fraction.

I am informed the federal government means to fix the weights and measures by a standard, which, like the coinage, will admit of the same *even* division by decimals. I am often asked why the English, after having proved the great utility of this scheme in their chain of one hundred links for land measuring, do not extend it to their coin, &c.? If you can think of a good solution to this question, pray let me have it in your next to

Yours sincerely, &c.

Philadelphia, August 18th, 1794.

DEAR SIR,

In a former letter I mentioned the relishes of salt fish usual at breakfast and supper in this country; they are chiefly of shad, a name given them by the first settlers, from their having *some resemblance* to that fish, though in fact they are very different; and indeed this is the case with almost every fish, bird, and other animal these Anglo-Americans took it into their heads to christen. It is a great pity they did not call those peculiar to this continent by their *indian* names; and this should also have been the case with mountains, lakes, rivers, &c. What man of any taste will not prefer the sonorous sounds of Susquana, Patapsico, Allegany, Raphanock, Potomack, and other *indian* titles, to such stupid appellations as Cape Cod, Mud Island, cat-fish, sheep's head-fish, whip poor will, &c.?

But to return to the *shad*, if it must be so called; it is an excellent fish, and comes up the rivers in prodigious shoals, in the months of April and May, to spawn. The largest nets used in this fishery are on the Delaware, where that river is from one to two miles wide. These nets are from one hundred and fifty to three hundred yards long. The greatest hawl ever known was upwards of nine thousand, from four to nine pounds per fish.

The revolution has not yet done away a fanatical law passed by the quakers, prohibiting the catching of these fish on a sunday; which, considering the short time they remain in the river, is highly impolitic.

There are thirteen fisheries within ten miles of Philadelphia; allowing only eight sundays in the season, and ten thousand shads lost in each of the twenty-four hours, a very moderate calculation, the aggregate loss to Philadelphia, and the adjacent country, is eighty thousand fish, weighing five pounds each, on an average. I say *loss*; for the return of the fish is the same now as it was a hundred and thirty years ago, when only a few dozen were taken in the season by the Indians.

There is also a small fish which comes up the rivers with the shad; the shoals this year have been uncommonly large; upwards of ten thousand have been taken at one hawl. Like the shad, it takes salt well; and, from it's having some resemblance to a *herring*, they give it that name, though very different from the herring which visits the shores of Europe. I believe there is no instance of a herring running a hundred and fifty miles up a fresh water river, or existing at all in water perfectly fresh.

The above particulars you may depend upon; they were communicated to me by Mr. West, who is proprietor of the largest shad-fisheries on the Delaware.

This river also abounds in cat-fish, perch, jack, eels, and a great variety of others; above all, in sturgeon; which are frequently caught by accident in the shad-nets, and either boiled for their oil, or suffered to rot on the, shores, being very seldom sent to market: when this is the case, they are sold for a mere trifle, chiefly to emigrants. The Americans have conceived a violent antipathy to this fish. I recollect no instance of seeing it at their tables. They have every externals appearance of the european sturgeon, but in other respects must be *very different*, or the Americans lose one of the best fisheries in the world.

Enclosed is an extract from general Lincoln's letter on the migration of fish. He endeavours to prove, that river fish, after their passage to the sea, whatever time they remain there, always return to the original waters in which they were spawned, unless some unnatural obstructions are thrown in their way.

Yours, &c.

In an old History of Bermuda, published in the year 1661, is the following passage: —

"There is great store of fish, which being mostly unknown to the English, they gave them such names as best *liked* them, as *porgie-fish, hog-fish, yellow-tails, cony-fish,* &c. "

EXTRACT.

"Whilst I resided in Philadelphia, in 1782, and 1783, I discovered that the shad brought to market from the Scuylkill were very superiour in flavour and firmness to those taken in the Delaware, which must proceed from their food in that river, previous to their going to the sea; as they are taken by the nets of the fishermen, before they are six hours in that river, on their return. I cannot think it a romantic idea, that the waters are impregnated with certain particles, on which they have been accustomed to feed; which is sufficient to allure them to where they were originally spawned; or that they are piloted there by some of the old fry. This idea will not appear improbable, when we consider the general laws which seem to control the whole finny tribe; and what would be the consequence should they be thrown down? The cod-fish which occupy the banks of Newfoundland, between the latitudes of 41 and 45, are very different, and are kept so distinct, and are so similar on the respective banks, that a man acquainted with that fishery will separate those caught on one bank from those of another, with as much ease as we separate the apple from the pear.

"I am, &c.

"Lincoln. "

Baltimore, 14th October, 1794.

DEAR FRIEND,

On the 7th of September I left the city of Brotherly Love, on my way to this town.

After sailing down the Delaware about two hours, in the water stage, our skipper run us on a sand bank. As there was no remedy but to wait patiently for the flow of tide, a party of us borrowed a boat, and went a shooting on the islands with which this part of the Delaware abounds. We landed at Fort Miflin, which was the principal obstruction to general Howe's progress up the river, in his way to Philadelphia, and obliged him to go several hundred miles round; this fort also kept the whole british fleet at bay, for some time after the army had taken possession of that city.

Fort Miflin, or Mud Fort (so called from it's low situation) is on an island in the Delaware, about one third nearer the Pennsylvania, than the Jersey shore.

During the first general attack of the british fleet the fort set fire to the Augusta, of 64 guns, and she shortly after blew up; and the Merlin sloop was so roughly handled, that she was hastily evacuated. The british admiral then procured a pilot, who carried two men of war, cut down for that purpose, on the Pennsylvania side of the island; a manoeuvre the Americans deemed impracticable. The works of the fort were now completely enfiladed, and on the 15th of November, the British began; a desperate attack, both from their ships on each side the island, and from a battery on the Pennsylvania shore.

The fort was supported by a battery on, the opposite side, and some row-gallies.

The british fire was heavy and well directed: they are supposed to have fired 1030 shots, weighing from 12 to 32 pounds, every 20 minutes, which, by the middle of the day, nearly levelled the works with the mud. This was the moment to storm the fort, which being lost by the British, the remains of the brave garrison made their retreat good to the Jersey shore the same night.

The British now having the complete command of the Delaware, totally dismantled this fort: in which state it remained till last year, when a french engineer was engaged to put it again into a state of defence. The works are already in great forwardness: the parapets are, according to the new french improvements, without embrasures, and the guns mounted on false carriages.

We also landed on several of, the other islands, and had tolerable sport.

At high water we proceeded on our voyage, and about twelve the next day arrived at Newcastle; whence I walked to Glasgow, a small village within a few miles of the river Elk, where general Howe landed his troops, after sailing two hundred and fifty miles up the bay of Chesapeak. His head quarters were at the house where I slept; the landlord also informed me, that I lay on the same bed general Washington occupied four times a year, in his way to his seat at Mount Vernon; an honour I did not *exactly* know the *value* of till the next morning, when he brought in *his bill*; after satisfying my conscientious landlord, I walked to French Town, which consists of *two houses*. This *town* is about 17 miles from the Delaware, and has a communication with the Chesapeak by means of the river Elk. But there is a nearer approximation of the Chesapeak to the Delaware, from a creek running into the latter at Apoquiminick, where the distance is only 7 miles: over this neck of land, all the trade between Philadelphia and Baltimore is conveyed in waggons. How soon would a canal be cut in such a situation in England!

I embarked in the Baltimore pacquet; had a pleasant sail down the Elk; in four hours entered the bay, and arrived here the same evening.

September 12th.

The yellow fever is certainly in town. Is it not astonishing the example of Philadelphia last year did not teach the inhabitants of Baltimore the necessity of building a lazaretto, and establishing a strict quarantine on all vessels from the infected islands in the West Indies? The first was not even attempted, and the last so carelessly performed, that I am mistaken if the fever has not been imported into more than *one* part of the town.

Sept. 29th. —The theatre closed at the request of the committee of health, the fever gaining ground rapidly, and the inhabitants quitting the town as fast as possible.

October the 2d.

The committee of health published their list of deaths, which they mean to continue every 24 hours. Died since the 1st of August 344 persons. The next day a violent cold and penetrating N. W. wind set in, with uncommon severity, which has entirely stopped the infection.

Oct. 14th. —The late cold weather has completely destroyed the yellow fever. The inhabitants are returned, and trade is restored to its usual course.

Yours, sincerely, &c.

* * * * *

Baltimore and the Point[Footnote: Or Fell's Point, the name given to a small but well-situated town about a mile lower down the bay.] may be considered but as one town, as the interval that parts them is already laid out for building.

There is not perhaps on the face of the earth so many excellent situations for a sea-port as in this vicinity; and yet they have fixed on the very spot where the town should *not* be.

Baltimore, by being built so far from the bay of Chesapeak, has not depth of water for a vessel of two hundred tons, nearer than the Point. The lower part of the town is a dead flat, intersected with canals and docks, filled with stagnated water from the Basin: owing to this circumstance the town is unhealthy at certain seasons, and subject, in the fall, to musquitoes: these inconveniences might have been avoided by building the town a mile lower, on either side the bay.

But there is a much better situation for a town and port on an inlet from the Patapsico, west of the town, round a point, which runs about W. N.W. where I have marked No. 10.

On this spot is water for a vessel of eight hundred tons burden, sufficiently fresh to exclude the worms, and at the same time a current strong enough to prevent stagnation. A bay perfectly secure from the N. W. and other dangerous winds, a gradual rise of ground consisting of a fine dry gravel to build upon; in short, every natural advantage. This was the original situation designed for the town; but the proprietor was concerned in a wharf in this neighbourhood, and fearing the new town would injure his business, positively refused his consent to the proposals made him on this occasion, and by that means, lost one of the first estates perhaps ever offered to an individual.

I was in this bay, on a fishing party, a few days ago, with one of his descendants, who was lamenting the infatuation of his ancestor. This gentleman was so kind as to point out and explain the foregoing particulars.

You will naturally inquire how the town came to be built in it's present situation? The governor of the province was proprietor of most of the land. Is not *that* a sufficient reason.

About forty years ago the two towns of Baltimore, and the Point, contained only *two* brick houses, and a few wooden ones: in a late edition of Salmon's Geography, I find Baltimore described as consisting of a few straggling houses, scarcely deserving the *name* of a *town*. Within these fifteen years it has increased in size and population beyond all precedent. It now contains nearly twenty thousand inhabitants; and, in point of trade, Baltimore is the fourth town in America.

The following anecdote will give you some idea of the growth of the town, and amazing increase in the value of land: —

An english gentleman, who emigrated to this country some years ago, built a small *country seat* on the side of the race ground; this house is now in the possession of a colonel Rogers, and in the *centre street of Baltimore*. The colonel has sold the wings for two thousand guineas to build upon, and still retains the house.

But the improvements have not advanced in proportion to the buildings; there is scarcely a dozen lamps in the whole town, which is badly paved, &c.

All the inhabitants agree as to the necessity of establishing a powerful, and energetic government, for the regulation of the town, *somewhere*; but though frequent town meetings have been called, they cannot agree about the *means*.

Something must soon be done, as the nuisances are every day increasing.

Yours sincerely, &c.

Since writing the above, the general assembly has ordered fifty thousand dollars be raised by lottery, which are laid out in paving the town, and clearing the Basin. Two enormous machines have been constructed on the dutch plan, to work with oxen, which make such progress in clearing the channel, that it is expected in a few years it will be sufficiently deep, to admit the largest merchantmen to come up to the wharfs of the town. And since my landing in England, my brother informs me, Baltimore is at last incorporated; a vigorous police established; and improvements are going on with spirit.

Baltimore, November 27th, 1794.

DEAR SIR,

Yours of the 21st of August I received. —So I find you fall into the commonplace notion of the English, that manufactories are forming here, which will in a short time render all importation of british goods unnecessary. Take my word for it, you have nothing of that kind to fear, whilst the United States have so few inhabitants, and so *much* of their best land uncultivated. It is not their *interest* to engage in manufactories; and when the country is sufficiently populous, it will be easier to conquer South America, and procure thence the *means* of purchasing commodities, than to go through the *drudgery* of their *fabrication*: but at present such is the cheapness of land, and the high price of wheat, and other produce, that it has raised the value of labour beyond the profits of almost any manufacture. If they could be established with effect in any part of America, it would be in the *New England states*, where the population is more than double those of the south; and provision much cheaper; but the New Englanders, when they fancy themselves too populous, rather than engage in a laborious trade, prefer emigration to the *Genasee*[Footnote: The Genasee is a rich tract of country, a considerable distance west of New York, much resorted to by New England emigrants since the peace with the Six Nations. Kentucky is at least one thousand miles from the nearest of the New England states, two hundred of which are through a wilderness, which cannot be passed during an indian war, without great danger.], or even Kentucky. The same restless, enterprising spirit, which brought their ancestors from Europe, carries them to these remote western settlements; and I have no doubt their descendants will continue the same in that direction; till the Pacific Ocean[Footnote: A distance of more than two thousand miles from the most remote western settlement.] stops their further progress; unless, as I before observed, lured by a *golden bait*, they go to the *south*: let the Spaniard look to that. —The manufactories in this country that have fallen under my observation are one of rifles at Lancaster, another of musquets at Connecticut, and at German Town, in Pennsylvania, a peculiar sort of winter stockings. An American has lately procured a patent from Congress, for cutting brads out of sheet iron with an engine. The american iron is of an excellent quality, and possesses a great degree of malleability, which perhaps suggested the first idea of this invention. The following extract from the advertisement of the patentee will enable you, to form some judgment of this singular undertaking: "He begs leave to observe their superiority to english-wrought brads consists in their being quite regular in their shape, so much so, that ten thousand may be drove through the thinnest pine board, without using a brad-awl, or splitting the board. They have the advantage also of being cut *with the grain* of the iron; others are cut *against* it. He has already three engines at work, which can turn out two hundred thousand per day. "

Another patent has been granted for making the teeth of cotton and wool cards by an engine, which is supposed to be a similar process.

There are also manufactories of cotton, sail cloth, gun-powder, glass, &c., but of no great consequence.

Their sawing-mills are numerous, and well constructed; this circumstance, and the great quantity of timber, mast, spars, &c., with which this country abounds, enable them to build vessels considerably under what you can afford in England, though the wages of a shipwright are now two dollars and a quarter per day. Theirs ships, in point of model and sailing, if not superiour, are at least equal to the best european-built vessels, and when constructed of *live oak*, and *red cedar*, are equally durable. Vessels of this description are scarce. Live oak is rarely met with north of the Carolinas: that used in the Boston ship-yards is brought from Georgia; a distance of more than a thousand miles,

Yours sincerely, &c.

Philadelphia, February 21st 1795.

DEAR SIR,

You know one motive for my coming to this country was, that I might have an unlimited range in my two favourite amusements, shooting, and fishing, and in both I have had tolerable sport. But as few except emigrants, follow the european method of shooting, I cannot purchase a pointer for any sum: pray send me one by an early fall ship, and if possible smuggle me half a dozen pounds of Battel powder; for since you have begun to cut one another's throats in Europe, I find it impossible to procure any but dutch, and that unglazed, at the *moderate* price of two dollars a pound.

We have two kinds of partridges; one larger, and the other smaller, than those of Europe: the former reside chiefly in the woods, and is in the southern states called a pheasant; but it is in fact neither one nor the other: the latter is called a quail in the northern states. The flesh of these birds is perfectly rich, white, and juicy, and though it has not a game flavour, is a very great delicacy. In other respects (except their size, and that they occasionally perch on the branches of a tree,) they differ very little in their plumage, call, manner of keeping in coveys, &c., from the partridge of England. They are amazingly prolific; I have often found twelve or fourteen coveys in the course of a few hours shooting; this will appear extraordinary, when you are informed there are no game laws in America, and that all ranks of citizens, or even a negro, may destroy them in any manner he pleases. When the snow is on the ground, whole coveys are taken in traps, and brought alive to market. They fly swiftly, and afford an excellent shot; but if the same covey be shot at a second time, they will often seek a refuge in the woods, whence it is difficult to dislodge them. They are very hardy, and will bear almost any degree of heat and cold; this circumstance, and their being so prolific, I should think would make a breed of them in England a very desirable acquisition. I am determined to bring over a few couples, by way of experiment.

We are visited by a sort of woodcock in July and August; we have also a kind of grouse, plover, dove, and wild pigeon, snipe, wild fowl, and a wonderful variety of small birds; among which, the *reed-bird* [Footnote: So called from their note resembling the word *reed.*], or american ortolan, justly holds the first place: they visit us from the south, and are found at certain seasons as far as the West Indies in that direction.

The back woodsmen, and indeed all western settlers, affect to despise our mode of shooting; they all use rifles, and throw a single ball to a great degree of certainty. The riflemen in the last war were all of this description, *Their* game are deer, bear, beaver, and other animals. The only *bird* they think worthy their attention is the wild turkey. An american naturalist (Bartram) says, "Our turkey of America is a very different species from the meleagris of Asia and Europe. I have seen several that have weighed between twenty and thirty pounds, and some have been killed that have weighed nearly forty pounds. "

Why do not the Americans domesticate this noble bird? They are much better adapted to bear this climate than the puny breed their ancestors imported from England. The few that are shot so far to the eastward as to be brought to our markets bear a great price.

The shooting of the back settlers is rather *business* than *sport*. When they are inclined for a frolic of the latter sort, they meet in large parties to shoot the gray squirrel: the devastation made on these occasions is incredible; the following is from the Kentucky Gazette; and I have no doubt, that it is strictly true: —

"*Lexington, July 13th.*

"At a squirrel-hunt in Madison county, on the 29th and 30th ult., the hunters rendezvoused at captain Archibald Wood's, and upon counting the *scalps*[Footnote: By scalp is here meant skin, which is an excellent fur.] taken, it was found they amounted to 5589! "

This sport is not confined to the back woods, but is in such general estimation, as to be preferred to all other shooting. They find this game by means of a mongrel breed of dogs, trained for that purpose; the squirrel, on being pursued, immediately ascends one of the most lofty trees he can find; the dog follows, and makes a point under the tree, looking up for his game. The squirrel hides himself behind the branches, and practises a thousand manoeuvres to avoid the shot; sometimes springing from one tree to another, with astonishing agility. Nature has given him a thick fur; this circumstance, and the height of the trees, make a long barrel, and large shot, indispensable in this kind of shooting. The best method of cooking the squirrel is in a ragout; this I learnt of a french epicure, who always speaks with rapture of this *bonne bouche*: it has a high game flavour, and is justly thought by the Americans to be an excellent dish; but we have many English, who, through mere prejudice, never tasted this animal; their antipathy also extends to bear, opossum, racoon, and cat-fish: —"Oh! " say the english ladies, "the *sight* of such frightful creatures is quite enough for me! "'

Fishing parties among the farmers, and in small towns in some parts of America, are very agreeably arranged: twelve or fourteen neighbours form themselves into a sort of club, and agree to fish one day in the week during the summer; previous: to which they fix on a romantic situation on the side of a wood commanding the intended scene of action. Under some of the large trees they erect a sort of hut, forming a dining-room and kitchen.

When the time is fixed to begin fishing, the steward for the day sends down a negro cook, with bread, butter, wine, liquors, culinary utensils, etc. About ten in the morning the fishermen arrive, and follow the sport in boats, canoes, or from the shore, either with angles or nets; but they seldom make use of the latter, except when they are disappointed in angling: they are then determined the fish, though not in a humour to bite, shall not deprive them of their dinner. At one they all meet at the place of general rendezvous, where all hands are employed in preparing the fish for the cook; by which means the dinner is soon on the table. —When over, and a few glasses have circulated, those who do not choose to remain drinking, take a nap during the heat of the day, which in this country is from two to four in the afternoon. At five the ladies arrive, and the company amuse themselves in catching fish for supper, walking in the woods, swinging, singing, playing on some musical instrument, &c. I have often been on these parties, and never spent my time more to my satisfaction; which is more than you will be able to say of that spent in reading this scrawl from

Yours, &c.

Travels in the United States of America

Philadelphia, May 7th, 1795.

DEAR SIR,

In answer so your last, respecting the aborigines of this continent, I am almost ashamed to inform you, I have scarcely any particulars on the subject worth troubling you with. Ever since my arrival in America, I have made up my mind to take the first opportunity of going to the westward on a shooting party, for a month or two, among the Indians; for which purpose I procured an introduction to the young *corn-planter*, son to a chief of the six nations, who is here for his education. He was no sooner informed of my intention, than he gave me a cordial invitation to attend him on his return in the fall; or, if I could not then make it convenient, at any other time; but the distance is so great, that, to confess the truth, I have never yet been able to raise the *necessary supplies*, and am likely to leave America without seeing a single wigwam.

The Indians have a fine natural genius for oratory, painting, and sculpture: I have a specimen of the latter cut with a knife on a piece of hickory, which is destitute neither of elegance of design, nor neatness of execution. But the most extraordinary trait in the character of these *red men* is their *continence*. We have every year fourteen or fifteen of their chiefs in this city, to form treaties, and other public business. They are often attended with well-made young men in the prime of life, and yet I never heard but of *one* instance of their engaging in a love-intrigue of *any kind*. They frequently tomahawk and scalp the most beautiful women, who are so unfortunate as to fall into their hands in time of war. —Each warrior cuts the number of scalps he has taken on his war club, and distinguishes the sex by certain marks. Several of these clubs, and other indian trophies taken from famous chiefs in former wars, are deposited in the Philadelphia Museum. On one war club I counted *five* fatal proofs of the savage who owned the weapon having butchered as many women!

But whatever cruelties they practise on their female captives, they are never known to take the slightest liberty with them *bordering on indecency*. Mary Rowlandson, a fanatic, who was captured in 1765, has the following passage in her narrative:

"I have been in the midst of these roaring lions, and savage bears, that neither fear God, man, nor devil, by day and night, *alone*, and in company, *sleeping all sorts together*, and yet not one of them offered me the least abuse of unchastity, in word or action! "

Charlevoix, in his account of the Canadian Indians, says, there is no example of their having taken the least liberty with any of the french women, even when their prisoners. In short, all accounts allow them this extraordinary male virtue, but differ whether it proceeds from education, or what the french call temperament.

But as they do not look upon chastity as a necessary requisite in the character of the squaws *before* marriage, these ladies are said by the white traders to be *less eminent* for this virtue than their warriors.

The works of F— — being little known in England, I send you some specimens of his writing on *indian* subjects; and, however uncouth, his language may appear, you may rely on the truth and accuracy of his descriptions: —

THE INDIAN STUDENT;
or,
FORCE OF NATURE.

RURA MIHI ET RIGUI PLACEANT IN VALLIBUS AMNES;
ILUMINA AMEM, SYLVASQUE INGLORIUS.

Virg. Georg. 2d. v. 483.

* * * * *

From Susquehanna's utmost springs,
  Where savage tribes pursue their game,
His blanket tied with yellow strings,
  A shepherd of the forest came.

Not long before, a wandering priest
  Express'd his wish with visage sad —
'Ah, why,' he cry'd, 'in Satan's waste,
  'Ah, why detain so fine a lad?

'In Yanky land there stands a town
  'Where learning may be purchas'd low —

46

'Exchange his blanket for a gown,
  'And let the lad to college go.'

From long debate the council rose,
  And viewing Shalum's tricks with joy,
To *Harvard hall*[1], o'er wastes of snows,
  They sent the copper-colour'd boy.
[Footnote 1: Harvard college, at Cambridge, near Boston.]

One generous chief a bow supply'd,
  This gave a shaft, and that a skin;
The feathers, in vermilion dy'd,
  Himself did from a turkey win:

Thus dress'd so gay, he took his way
  O'er barren hills, alone, alone!
His guide a star, he wander'd far,
  His pillow every night a stone.

At last he came, with leg so lame,
  Where learned men talk heathen Greek,
And hebrew lore is gabbled o'er,
  To please the muses, twice a week.

A while he writ, a while he read,
  A while he learn'd the grammar rules.—
An indian savage, so well bred,
  Great credit promis'd to their schools.

Some thought, he would in law excel,
  Some said, in physic he would shine;
And one, that knew him passing well,
  Beheld in him a sound divine.

But those of more discerning eye,
  E'en then could *other* prospects show,
And saw him lay his Virgil by,
  To wander with his dearer *bow*.

The tedious hours of study spent,
  The heavy-moulded lecture done,
He to the woods a hunting went,
  But sigh'd to see the setting sun.

No mystic wonders fir'd his mind;
  He sought to gain no learn'd degree,
But only sense enough to find
  The *squirrel in the hollow tree.*

The shady bank, the purling stream,
  The woody wild his heart possess'd;
The dewy lawn his morning dream
  In fancy's gayest colours dress'd.

'And why,' he cried, 'did I forsake
  My native wood for gloomy walls?
The silver stream, the limpid lake,
  For musty books and college halls?

'A little could my wants supply—
  Can wealth and honour give me more?
Or, will the sylvan god deny
  The humble treat he gave before?

'Let seraphs reach the bright abode,
  And Heav'n's sublimest mansions see:—
I only bow to Nature's God—
  The land of shades, will do for *me.*

'These dreadful secrets of the sky
  'Alarm my soul with chilling fear:—
'Do planets in their orbits fly?
  'And is the Earth, indeed, a sphere?

'Let planets still their aim pursue,
  'And comets round creation run—
'In Him my faithful friend I view,
  'The image of my God—the Sun.

'Where Nature's ancient forests grow,
  'And mingled laurel never fades,
'My heart is fix'd; and I must go
  'To die among my native shades.'

He spoke,—and to the western springs
  (His gown discharged, his money spent)
His blanket tied with yellow strings,

The shepherd of the forest went.

Returning to the rural reign,
  The Indians welcom'd him with joy;
The council took him home again,
  And bless'd the copper-coloured boy.

Our author, brings his hero again upon the stage, under the title of

THE SPLENETIC INDIAN.

"To the best of my recollection, it was about the middle of the month of August; we were sitting on a green bank by the brook side; the fox grapes were not yet come to maturity; but we were anticipating the pleasure we should soon experience in eating some fine clusters, that at this instant hung over our heads in the tall shade of a beech tree; when, upon a sudden clamour raised by some young fellows, who were advancing rapidly towards us, the learned Indian sachem Tomo-cheeki, who at this time happened to be my friend and companion, seized me by the hand, and intimated a strong desire, that I should accompany him to his *wigwam*, situate at many miles distance in the wilderness.

"A request so unusual, and at such a sultry season of the year (it being now the height of the dog days), and to all appearance occasioned by so trifling a circumstance as the approach of a few noisy bacchanalians, could not but give me some surprise. I nevertheless accepted his offer, and we then walked on together westward, without saying a word, though not forgetting to kindle our pipes afresh at the first house we came to.

"We had no sooner entered the forest, than I began to be convinced, that all things around us were precisely such as nature had finished them; the trees were straight and lofty, and appeared as if they had never been obliged to art in their progress to maturity; the streams of water were winding and irregular, and not odiously drawn into a right line by the spade of the ditcher. The soil had never submitted to the ploughshare, and the air that circulated through this domain of nature was replete with that balmy fragrance, which was breathed into the lungs of the long-lived race of men, that flourished in the first ages of the world.

"At last we approached the wigwam, as I discovered by the barking of a yellow dog, who ran out to meet us. The building seemed to be composed of rough materials, and at most was not more than eight feet in height, with a hole in the centre of the roof, to afford a free passage to the smoke from within. It was situate in a thicket of lofty trees, on the side of a stream of clear water, at a considerable distance from the haunts of civilized men. A young indian girl was angling in the deepest part of the stream, whence she every now and then drew a trout, or some other inhabitant of the waters. An old squaw sat at a very small distance, and, after cutting off the heads, and extracting the entrails, hung the fish in the smoke, to preserve them against the time of winter.

"The Indian and myself then entered the wigwam, and without ceremony seated ourselves on blocks of wood covered with fox skins. The furniture of his habitation consisted of scarcely any thing besides. The flooring was that which was originally common to all men and animals. I thought myself happy, that I had been permitted to come into the world, in an age when some vestige of the primitive men, and their manners of living, were yet to be found. A few ages will totally obliterate the scene.

"I now determined to teaze the Indian, if possible—'But for a man of your education, ' says I, 'sachem Tomo-cheeki; to bury yourself in this savage retreat, is to me inexplicable. You who have travelled on foot no less than one hundred and seventeen leagues, till you reached the walls of Havard college, and all for the sake of gaining an insight into languages, arts, and mysteries; and then to neglect all you have acquired at last, is a mode of conduct, for which I cannot easily account—What! was not the mansion of a fat *clergyman* a more desirable acquisition than this miserable hut, these gloomy forests, and yonder savage stream? —Were not the food and liquor belonging to the white men of the *law* far superiour to these insipid fish, these dried roots, and these running waters? —Were not a *physician's* cap, an elegant morning gown, and a grave suit of black clothes, made by an european tailor, more tempting to your imagination, than this wretched blanket, that is eternally slipping from your shoulders, unless it be fastened with skewers, which are by no means convenient? '

"Pardon me, ' replied the Indian, 'if all those blessings and advantages you have mentioned seemed nothing to my view, in comparison with these *divine solitudes*: opinion alone is happiness.

The *Great Man*, who has chosen his habitation beyond the stars, will dispose of us as he pleases. I am under an obligation of passing happily here that life which he has given me, because in so doing I serve and adore him. I could not but be sorrowful, were I to be removed for ever from this stream. Let me alone, white man; others shall make laws, and pass sleepless nights, for the advantage of the world; sachem Tomo-cheeki will leave all things to the *invisible direction*; and, provided he can be contented in his *wigwam*, the end of his existence is accomplished.

"But, ' continued he, 'of what great value can that education be, which does not inculcate moral and social *honesty* as it's first and greatest principle. The knowledge of all things above and below is of inconsiderable worth, unconnected with the heart of rectitude and benevolence. —Let us walk to the remains of an old indian town; the bones of my ancestors repose in its vicinity. ' —

"He had scarcely uttered these words when he seized his staff, and rushed out of the wigwam with a sort of passionate violence, as if deeply agitated at the recollection of the past, present, and future fate of his countrymen. —I followed him with equal celerity. 'But, ' said he, 'it is in vain to grieve! In three centuries there will not be one individual of all our race existing upon the Earth. I lately passed this stream, and it being swollen with rains at my return, I could not without the greatest danger cross over it again to my wigwam; the winds raged, the rain fell, and the storms roared around me. I laid me down to sleep beneath a copse of hazles. Immediately the unbodied souls of my ancestors appeared before me. Grief was in their countenances. All fixed their eyes upon me, and cried, one after the other, "*Brother, it is time thou hadst also arrived in our abodes: thy nation is extirpated, thy lands are gone, thy choicest warriors are slain; the very wigwam in which thou residest is mortgaged for three barrels of hard cider! Act like a man, and if nature be too tardy in bestowing the favour, it rests with yourself to force your way into the invisible mansions of the departed. "*

"By this time we had arrived at the ruins of the old indian town. The situation was highly romantic, and of that kind which naturally inclines one to be melancholy. At this instant a large heavy cloud obscured the sun, and added a grace to the gloominess of the scene. The vestiges of streets and squares were still to be traced; several favourite trees were yet standing, that had outlived the inhabitants; the stream ran, and the springs flowed, as lively as ever, that had afforded refreshment to so many generations of men, that were now passed away, never to return. All this while the Indian had melancholy deeply depicted in his countenance; but he did not shed many tears, till we came to that quarter where his ancestors had been entombed. 'This spot of land, ' said he, recovering himself a little, 'was once sacred to the dead; but it is now no longer so! This whole town, with a large tract around it, not even excepting the bones of our progenitors, has been sold to a stranger. We were deceived out of it, and that by a man who understood Greek and Hebrew; five kegs of whiskey did the business: he took us in the hour of dissipation, when the whole universe appeared to us but a little thing; how much less then, this comparatively small tract of country, which was, notwithstanding, our whole dependance for the purposes of hunting and fishing! — —Here, ' continued he, sighing, 'was the habitation of *Tawlongo*, one of our most celebrated warriors. He, in his time, could boast of having gained no fewer than one hundred and twenty-seven complete victories over his enemies; yet he was killed at last by an unarmed *Englishman*.

"Here, too, on the opposite side of the way, stood the house of *Pilaware*, the admirable; she had been addressed by thirty-three suitors of her own nation, but refused them all, and went off at last with an *irish pedlar*, for the sake of three yards of silver riband, and a new blanket. Yonder stood the dwelling of *Scuttawabah*, my immediate ancestor; he died for joy of having found a keg of rum, that had been lost by some western trader. May his joys be continued behind the western mountains—Recollection overcomes me—Let us return to the wigwam in the forest. '

"As soon as we had reached this sequestered abode, the Indian once more sat himself down, and leaned his head upon his hand, melancholy enough, to be sure.

"The old squaw desired to know why he was so sorrowful—The *remedy*, ' said she, *is in your power.* '—He then started up, as if suddenly recollecting somewhat, and cried out, 'Existence is but a dream, an agreeable dream indeed, if we only choose to consider it as such. —Bring me that jug of strong cider; it will be my friend, when all others fail and forsake me—Choicest gift of God to man! and which the white people alone possess the art and knowledge of producing! '—He courteously offered me a share of his beverage; but I found it so intolerably sour, that I was forced to swear by all the gods of the Indians, I would not have any connexion with it. —He then pointed to the stream where the girl was angling, and said, with a peasant countenance that had brightened up for a moment, 'Go; you are a *sober* man; the clear waters are good for you; for my own part, this juice of the apple shall be sufficient. '—Two hours now elapsed, without any one uttering a word. —The Indian had by this time drunk two large gallons of cider; and recollecting in an instant, he had signed away his lands and wigwam, some days before, for a *mere trifle*, he became at once outrageous; his rage heightened to an alarming degree of extravagance by the strong fumes of the liquor he had swallowed. —'*It is enough,* ' said he; '*my house and lands are departed: I will speak a word in favour of suicide.*

"'Tis all in vain! These flowers, these streams, these solitary shades, are nothing to me. I shall not offend the spirit of truth when I say, they are odious in my eyes. Sixty times has the sun performed his journey of a year, since I was first struck with the beauty of his yellow rays. Could I be a witness of sixty yet to come, would there be any thing new, or which I had not seen before? It is high time we should intrude ourselves into the invisible abodes, when all things satiate and grow stale upon us here below. I will this very night enclose myself in my wigwam, and, setting it on fire, depart with the thin vapour that shall arise from the dried wood of the forest, when piled around me—No, no, ' continued he, tasting the remains of his cider '*there is nothing new;* all is *old, stale; and insipid.* '

"At this instant an Indian trader alighted at the door. He appeared to have come a considerable distance, and now proffered to barter a keg of *french brandy* for some beaver skins, he saw hanging out a post.

"French brandy! ' cried Tomo cheekily 'that must be something *new.*'

"It is surely such, ' replied the wandering trader, 'at least in this remote wilderness. '

"I will taste it, by Heaven, ' said the Indian.

"But will it not prove the falsehood of your position and assertion, ' interrupted I, 'that there is nothing *new under the sun? To him that exists through all ages nothing can be strange or novel; with the transitory race of man, the case is wholly different. Art and Nature are combined in perpetually composing new forms and substances for his use and amusement on the ocean of life.* '

"The Divinity himself must surely reside in that precious liquor! ' exclaimed the Indian, after tasting it a second time; 'take all my skins and furs; and when the dawn of the morning appears, return home, stranger, and bring a fresh supply of this celestial beverage. My existence had indeed begun to be a burden: I was meditating, to extricate myself by the shortest method. I have now learned wisdom, and am convinced, that it is *variety alone that can make life desirable.* "

* * * * *

In order to understand the following, I must inform you, F—— had been telling the story of a love-distracted maid, somewhat similar to Sterne's Maria. You will suppose her lately to have put an end to her existence. —

"We had not proceeded very far on our way, when we discovered a funeral procession advancing towards us, headed by the parson of the parish in which we were. He was a little man, dressed in black, with a scarf hanging over his left shoulder. —Upon inquiry, we found they were proceeding to a church about a league distant, where the corpse they attended was to be deposited.

"And to whom may this body belong? " said the *indian physician,* addressing the man who walked in the rear of the procession.

"It is the corpse of the unfortunate Marcia, ' replied the other, speaking low; 'she died suddenly, yesterday morning, and is now carrying to be interred in the vault of her ancestors. ' We were much affected at this intelligence, as we had hoped to hear of her recovery, instead of her decease.

"At the request of my friend, the man in the white linen coat, the Indian agreed to attend the funeral along with us, and accordingly we all three fell in among the followers, and travelled on with a slow pace till we came to the scene of interment. The situation was wild and gloomy. Naked rocks, dark cedars, the head of a small lake, and the venerable tombs of the dead, completed the scenery.

"It was pity, ' said I, 'to the singing clerk, who stood near me, 'that Fate has so ordered matters, that this young creature should depart the world in so very extravagant a condition of mind. Though too many pass their whole lives in a state of insanity, it were to be wished, that, towards the evening, the clouds of phrensy might be dissipated, and the sun of reason set clear. '

"The singing clerk looked full in my face, opened his mouth wide, and was about to make some reply, when silence was ordered, that the clergyman might pronounce a speech over the body; but his reverence stumbled at the threshold: he had unluckily forgot his pocket Bible, and could not recollect his *text*.

"Cannot he say something applicable to the melancholy occasion, ' whispered the Indian, 'without the formality of taking a *text*? '

"Were you to give him three worlds, each as rich as a dozen of the Indies, ' replied the clerk, 'you could not get a word out of him on any other condition. '

"The sexton of the parish was then ordered to mount one of the horses, and make the best of the way to the good doctor's house, to bring the Bible.

"After waiting a full and entire hour, he returned with the vexatious intelligence, that the Bible was not to be found—it was stolen—or, it was hid—or it had been *neglected*—or, it was mislaid—or they knew not what had been done with it. —'More is the pity! ' exclaimed the singing clerk.

"The doctor of divinity then mounted the horse himself, apparently with some uneasiness, and set out personally to bring the Bible at all events.

"By this time, however, the sun was set, and the whole company stood waiting in anxious expectation of the clergyman's return, till darkness had taken possession of the earth; but there was yet no appearance of either the divine or his Bible.

"As it is more than probable he cannot find his book, ' said the man in the white linen coat, 'I am positive he will not return at all; and, as it is now almost dark, I am of opinion the sooner the funeral ceremonies are finished the better. The body of the unfortunate Marcia ought not to be deposited in these silent retreats of death without some living token of our respect. She was amiable while living, and notwithstanding the misfortune of a disordered brain, and an innocent, unsuspecting confidence in another's honour, is, in my way of thinking, no less amiable when dead. —Our friend, the Indian will, I know, be complaisant enough on this occasion to give us a few sentences, and then the venerable sexton may proceed to close the scene, and we shall be at liberty to return to our respective homes. '

"This man is not in holy orders, ' cried the sexton.

"He does not wear a black coat or gown, ' said the singing clerk.

"He has not a gray wig on his head, observed one of the church wardens.

"It is no matter, ' replied the man in the white linen coat, 'he has a plain understanding, has written a treatise on the virtues of tobacco, and knows what is common sense, as well as the best of you. '

"Casting my eyes at this instant toward the east, I perceived a glimmering among the trees, which proved to be the moon rising, two days after the full. The evening was calm and serene, and every thing was hushed, except the surge of the ocean, which we could distinctly hear breaking on the rocks of the adjacent coasts; when, finding the parish clergyman did not return, the Indian shook the dew from his blanket, stepped boldly upon a tombstone of black marble, and, for reasons best known to himself, preferring the Indian style on this occasion, he thus began: —

"Instead of these dismal countenances, why have we not a feast of seven days? Instead of the voice of sorrow, why are not the instruments of music touched by the hand of skill? Fair daughter of the morning! thou didst not perish by slow decay. At the rising of the sun we saw thee; the ruddy bloom of youth was then upon thy countenance; In the evening thou wert nothing; and the pallid complexion of death had taken place of the bloom of beauty. —And now thou art gone to sit down in the gardens that are found at the setting of the sun, behind the western mountains, where the daughters of the white men have a separate place allotted to them by the spirit of the hills. As much as the mind is superiour to the body, so much are those charming regions preferable to these which we now inhabit. Man is here but an image of himself, the representation of an idea that in itself is not subjected to a change. That which derived it's origin from the dust shall indeed to the dust return; but the fine ethereal substance does not cease to think, and shall be again employed by the immortal gods to put the forms of things in motion. What was thine errour? —It was nothing: the bow was too mighty for the string, and the foundation too feeble for the fabric that was built upon it. All shall be right when thou art arrived at the foot of the mountains, where the sound of the wintry winds will not be permitted to reach thee, and where the light of the lamp is not extinguished by the sickly blasts of autumn. — —

"*What infernal stuff is this?* ' exclaimed the clergyman, who at this period of the Indian's discourse had returned on a full gallop with a large folio Bible before him: '*what infernal heretical trash is this, with which my ears are insulted? —Miscreant, avaunt!* ' said he, addressing the Indian, '*or I will teach you how to make speeches within the bounds of my jurisdiction,* '

"The Indian then modestly stepped down from the tombstone, and the legitimate clergyman took his place. After making a slight apology for his stay, he read his text by the light from a horn lantern, which the clerk held up to his nose, and then proceeded to mumble over a written discourse upon the subject he had chosen, and which held him about half an hour. —'In my country, ' observed the Indian, 'they would make a more *animated* speech at the interment of a *favourite racoon!* '

"'This divinity-monger is the angel of our church, ' answered the man in the white linen coat; 'and it is dangerous to criticise upon his productions, especially as he considers every one to be in the wrong, who does not precisely fall in with his own opinions in matters appertaining to religion. '

"'Weak men are always arrogant, positive, and self-conceited, ' replied the Indian.

"'Let us hasten home, ' whispered the man in the white linen, coat, 'for the night begins to wear apace. "

* * * * *

Before the following lines are read, represent to yourself, that some of the tribes of Indians bury their dead in a sitting posture. —

LINES
OCCASIONED BY A VISIT TO
AN OLD INDIAN BURYING-GROUND.

In spite of all the learn'd have said,
  I still my old opinion keep,
The *posture* that *we* give the dead,
  Points out the soul's eternal sleep.

Not so the ancients of these lands:—
  The Indian, when from life releas'd,
Again is seated with his friends,
  And shares again the joyous feast.

His imag'd birds, and painted bowl,
  And ven'son for a journey drest,
Bespeak the *nature* of the soul—
  Activity, that wants no rest.

His bow for action ready bent,
  And arrows with a head of bone,
Can only mean that life is spent,
  And not the finer essence gone.

Thou, stranger, that shalt come this way,
  No fraud upon the dead commit;
Yet, mark the swelling turf, and say,
  'They do not *lie*, but here they *sit*'

Here still a lofty rock remains,
  On which the curious eye may trace
(Now wasted half by weiring rains)
  The fancies of a ruder race.

Here still an aged elm aspires,
  Beneath whose far projecting shade
(And which the shepherd still admires)
  The children of the forest play'd.

There oft a restless indian queen,
  (Pale Marian, with her braided hair)
And many a barb'rous form, is seen,
  To chide the man that lingers there.

By midnight moons, o'er moist'ning dews,
  In vestments for the chace array'd,
The hunter still the deer pursues—
  The hunter and the deer—a shade.

And long shall tim'rous fancy see
  The painted chief, and pointed spear,
And, *Reason's self* shall bow the knee
  To shadows and delusions here.

Philadelphia, September 22d, 1795.

DEAR SIR,

I find from a perusal of the english papers, that fencibles are raising in all parts of the country, and every precaution taking, to put the kingdom in the best state of defence, in case of an invasion. I have for some years thought a few regiments of riflemen would much contribute to this desirable end.

Some lessons I have received in the use of the rifle, from back woodsmen, since my arrival in America, have confirmed me in this opinion.

I know it will be objected, that the rifle is not a fair weapon. Perhaps it is not. —I should be sorry to see it in general use in the european armies: but surely it may be used to repel an invader, without any infringement of the Law of Nations.

What I would recommend to Government on this subject is, first,

OF FORMING THE CORPS.

Beside the officers who have paid any attention to this method of fighting during the last war in America, some of the most experienced back woodsmen and indian chiefs should be sent for from Canada.

Independent of the regiments on the ordinary establishment, I would recommend one of *select men*, with better pay, &c., to be formed from the other rifle corps; *merit* being the only recommendation.

Volunteer companies, in different parts of the country, might soon be formed, composed of gentlemen, sportsmen, gamekeepers, &c. Proper persons should make the circuit of the kingdom, to instruct them in some of the most necessary particulars; such as loading, with the proper use of the patch; to draw a level, making a just allowance for distance, &c.

OF RIFLES.

I would by no means recommend *contract* let proper encouragement be given to gun-smiths, to supply rifles of the best construction, *loading from the muzzle.* —Their being of an uniform length, or bore, is of no consequence, as every man should cast and cut his own ball.

The barrel, mounting, and lock, should be covered with a composition, to render them as dull, and as little discernible, as possible. The locks should always be in the very best firing order, and constructed to give fire as easily as the nature of the service will admit. Oil, for the inside of the rifle, should be regularly served; and the flints should be of a much better quality than those used in muskets.

POWDER.

Every thing depends upon this article's being of an uniform degree of strength: it should be of the best quality, but not glazed.

ACCOUTREMENTS AND DRESS,

Cannot be better than those used by the rifle corps in this country, except perhaps that the latter should be of a dusky green, the colour died in the Highlands of Scotland for plaids; even the cap should be of this colour: a sort of helmet, constructed so as to afford a rest to fire from, when lying on the belly.

EXERCISE, &c.

It may perhaps be presumption in me to say any thing on this subject; but I cannot help thinking it should be the *reverse* of what is used in the Line. They should be encamped as much as possible in a woody country, as the art of *freeing,* as the back woodsmen call it, is one of their best manoeuvres. Their whole time should be taken up in the *real* study of their profession, not in powdering, pipeclaying, blacking, polishing, and such military fopperies.

The rifle out of the question, I do not think *slow, deliberate firing* sufficiently attended to in the english army. Want of ammunition first introduced it into this country at Bunker's Hill, and afterward at Sullivan's Island. The carnage that ensued was a fatal proof of it's efficacy.

I have often thought, that the success of our navy was in a great measure owing to *cool, deliberate firing;* and there is no doubt but that the military fame of our ancestors was owing to their great superiority in shooting the long bow; for the exercise of which, butts were erected in every village in the kingdom. —

From

Yours, &c

.

Philadelphia, February 12th, 1796.

DEAR FRIEND,

Were I to characterise the *United States*, it should be by the appellation of the *land of speculation*.

Such has been the rapid rise of every article of american produce, of house-rent, and land (to say nothing of mercantile speculation, great part of the carrying trade of Europe being now in the hands of the Americans), that surely there never was a country where that passion was so universal, or had such unbounded scope.

The last great purchase of land from the Indians, on the confines of Georgia, was at the rate of a cent per acre; one hundred acres for a dollar!

Before the american war, flour, was sold at *two* dollars, per barrel; it is now selling at *fourteen*.

But perhaps the most tempting speculation is that of the *mines*. Our friend, Parsons, who is here looked upon as an agent to some english speculators, has lately received the enclosed, which I begged a copy of, for your perusal but should first inform you, the cheapest fuel you can burn in some parts of America, is english coal from Liverpool!

Farewell.

COPY OF A LETTER TO B. PARSONS.

"SIR,

"The coal mine, of which you requested, me to give you a description, is situate in the county of Hampshire, on a spur or arm of the Allegany mountains. At the foot of this, within the distance of one mile, is the river Patowmack, at the confluence of it's north branch with the Savage river. To this point, the Patowmack Company, incorporated for this purpose, intend to extend their navigation, and have already perfected it within the distant of six or seven miles. The work is going forward, and I believe will be completed next summer. This being perfected, there will be a good navigation for large flat-bottomed boats, within one mile of the coal-bank, to which a good road may be had on the side of the mountain.

"This immense body of coal, which lies not above two or three feet under the surface of the earth, was discovered by the falling of a tree, the roots of which brought up some pieces of coal. It has been made use of for some years by the neighbouring blacksmiths, who have made a perpendicular opening, about ten feet on this side of the mountain. Intending to purchase this property, I employed a man about two years ago to dig about twelve feel lower down than the first opening, and found nothing but a solid body of coal, of an excellent quality. I am inclined to think it extends to the bottom of the mountain, and may be procured with so much ease, that one hand, as I am assured, could deliver three hundred bushels a day.

"From the information I have received, there is a body of iron ore within seven or eight miles of the coal-bank; and I expect a very advantageous situation for water-works might be found at the confluence of the North Branch and the Savage. Among the great objects contemplated by the Patowmack Company in clearing the navigation of that extensive river, was that of forming an easy communication between the eastern and western waters, which you know are divided by the Allegany Mountains. The space that separates them at present is about sixty miles; but when the obstructions to the navigation down the Patowmack, which, passing through an extensive and fertile country, leads to the seat[Footnote: The writer means *intended* seat of federal empire.] of federal empire; and thence widening by degrees to the width of twelve miles, empties itself into the bay of Chesapeak.

"Should any of your friends in England incline to form an establishment here, in the smaller branches of non manufactory, I should he glad to treat with them on terms mutually beneficial.

"Yours, &c. "

Philadelphia June 27th, 1796.

DEAR FRIEND,

"In some part of the middle states, a climate similar to that of England may easily be found. "

Inform our old acquaintance H— —, that if he emigrates to America on the strength of this assertion of Cooper, (on which, you tell me he so much depends), he will, on his arrival, find himself egregiously mistaken. The sameness of latitude does not always indicate similarity of temperature: there are many other causes, which contribute to make this a very different climate from that of Great Britain.

The middle states of North America are hotter and colder *at intervals*, not only than England, but than any part of the Old Continent, under the same parallel of latitude.

Jefferson says, "Our changes from heat to cold are sudden and great. The mercury in Fahrenheit's thermometer has been known to descend from 92 to 47, in thirteen hours. "

And I copied the following from a New York paper: —

"Wednesday, the 14th of May, the mercury in Fahrenheit rose to 91 degrees, The Saturday night following, there was a severe frost. The next Tuesday and Wednesday, the mercury rose to 85 degrees; from the 20th to the 26th, it has been nearly stationary, varying only from 60 to 64. : Easterly wind, and rain. "

These violent transitions from heat to cold, are produced by means of the N. W. wind, which in this country is the most keen and severe of any that is to be met with on the face of the globe. It is much the most prevalent wind we have, and seldom fails to blow four or five days with great uniformity. This wind is perfectly *dry*, and so uncommonly penetrating, that I am convinced it would destroy all the plagues of Egypt in a very short time. You may recollect, I informed you of the astonishing effect of this powerful agent in stopping the yellow fever in a few hours, last year, at Baltimore.

Neither the prevalence, nor uncommon severity of this wind has been properly accounted for; but we may now expect something more satisfactory on this subject, from the celebrated Volney; who is here endeavouring to investigate the causes of this, and other phenomena, relative to the winds of this continent.

Our heats in summer are sometimes very great; but the excess seldom exceeds three days; the rotation is generally as follows; the first day perhaps the mercury rises to 86, the next to 90, and the 3rd to 97, and sometimes, though very rarely, to upward of 100 then comes a thunder gust, which restores the air to it's usual summer temperature, till another three days period of excessive heat begins and ends in the same manner, at intervals, through the season. The succession of the degree of cold in winter is exactly the same: I never knew the excess exceed three days; not that we have then a thaw but that the weather is moderate, till another excess commences of three days.

On these occasions the mercury *sometimes* descends to 10 or 12 degrees below 0. Rivers a mile broad are frozen over in one night, and the bay of Chesapeak traversed in waggons and sleighs!

Though this climate, compared with that of England, is not in my opinion on the whole so good, yet it possesses many advantages, such as the clearness of the atmosphere, greater equality of the length of the days, and *certainty* of settled weather; for though the transitions are more *violent*, they are by no means so *frequent* as in England; where you have the wind from every point of the compass, and experience all the seasons of the year in twenty-four hours!

Recollect these observations on the climate of America are confined to the *middle states*, including Virginia in this description. Those of the north, and south, are *somewhat* different; but I am informed the country to the S. W. of the Allegany Mountains is *materially different*. The distance the N. W. wind has to travel to this country, and the opposition it meets with from those mountains, in a great measure meliorates and destroys those penetrating qualities, which make this wind so formidable to the Atlantic States. I have heard so many extraordinary accounts of the South-western territory, that I have long made up my mind to visit that country: two *trifling* reasons alone prevented me; viz. want of *time* and *money*; and from some disagreeable intelligence I have lately received from *Wells*, instead of climbing the *Allegany,* I apprehend I shall soon be obliged to cross the *Atlantic;* in which case, I shall have the pleasure of returning you thanks in person for your obliging attention to my order concerning the........... which I received by the Peggy.

At present I must content myself by assuring you of my being

Your obliged friend, &c.

Philadelphia, September 13th, 1796.

DEAR SIR,

I write this in my way to Boston, where I am going to fulfil my engagement with W——, the particulars of which I informed you of in a former letter.

When I arrived at Newcastle, I had the mortification to find upwards of one hundred irish passengers on board the packet.

For some time before I left Baltimore, our papers were full of a shocking transaction, which took place on board an irish passenger ship, containing upwards of three hundred. It is said, that, owing to the cruel usage they received from the captain, such as being put on a *very scanty* allowance of water[Footnote: By a law of the United States, the quantity of water and provision every vessel is obliged to take (in proportion to the length of the passage and persons on board) is clearly defined. A master of a vessel violating this law forfeits five hundred dollars.] and provision, a contagious disorder broke out on board, which carried off great numbers; and, to add to their distress, when they arrived in the Delaware, they were obliged to perform quarantine, which, for some days, was equally fatal.

The disorder was finally got under by the physicians belonging to the Health Office. We had several of the survivors on board, who confirmed all I had heard: indeed their emaciated appearance was a sufficient testimony of what they had suffered. They assured me, the captain sold the ship's water by the pint; and informed me of a number of shocking circumstances, which I will not wound your feelings by relating.

It is difficult to conceive how a multitude of witnesses can militate *against* a fact; but more so, how three hundred passengers could tamely submit to such cruelties, from a bashaw of a captain.

I am happy to inform you the Philadelphia Hibernian Society are determined to prosecute this *flesh butcher* for *murder*; As the manner of carrying on this *trade* in human flesh is not generally known in England, I send you a few particulars of what is here emphatically called a *white Guinea man*. There are vessels in the trade of Belfast, Londonderry, Amsterdam, Hamburgh, &c., whose chief *cargoes*, on their return to America, are passengers; great numbers of whom, on their arrival, are *sold* for a term of years to pay their passage; during their servitude, they are liable to be *resold*, at the death or caprice of their masters. Such advertisements as the following, are frequent: —

"To be disposed of, the indentures of a strong, healthy, *irish woman*; who has two years to serve, and is fit for all kind of house work. — Enquire of the printer. "

"Stop the villain!

Ran away this morning, an irish servant, named Michael Day, by trade a tailor, about five feet eight inches high, fair complexion, has a down look when spoken to, light bushy hair, speaks much in the irish dialect, &c. :—Whoever secures the above described, in any gaol, shall receive thirty dollars reward, and all reasonable charges paid. —N. B.. All masters of vessels are forbid harbouring, or carrying off the said servant at their peril. "

The laws respecting the *redemptioners*[Footnote: The name given to these persons.] are very severe; they were formed for the english convicts before the revolution. There are lately hibernian, and german societies, who do all in their power, to mitigate the severity of these laws, and render their countrymen, during their servitude, as comfortable as possible. These societies are in all the large towns south of Connecticut. In New England they are not wanting, as the *trade* is there prohibited. The difficulty of hiring a tolerable servant induces many to *deal* in this way. Our friend S— — lately bought an irish girl for three years, and in a few days discovered he was likely to have a greater *increase of his family* than he bargained for; we had the laugh sadly against him on this occasion; I sincerely believe the jew regrets his new purchase is not a few shades darker. If he could prove her a *women of colour*, and produce a bill of sale, he would make a slave of the child as well as the mother! The emigration from Ireland has been this year very great; I left a large *vessel*[Footnote: These vessels frequently belong to Philadelphia, but land their passengers here, as there is a direct road to the back parts of Pennsylvania.] full of passengers from thence at Baltimore: I found *three* at Newcastle: and there is *one* in this city. The number of passengers cannot be averaged at less than two hundred and fifty to each vessel, all of whom have arrived within the last six weeks!

While the yellow fever was raging in this city, in the year 1793, when few vessels would venture nearer than Fort Miflin; a german captain in *this trade* arrived in the river, and hearing that such was the fatal nature of the infection, that a sufficient number of nurses could not be procured to attend the sick for any sum, conceived the philanthropic idea of supplying this deficiency from his *redemption passengers!* actuated by this *humane motive,* he sailed boldly up to the city, and *advertised*[Footnote: I have preserved this advertisement, and several others equally curious.] his *cargo* for sale: —

"A few *healthy* servants, generally between seventeen and twenty-one years of age; their times will be disposed of, by applying on board the brig. "

Generous soul! thus nobly to sacrifice his *own countrymen, pro bono publico.* I never heard this *honest* german was *properly* rewarded; but virtue is it's own reward, and there is no doubt but the consciousness of having performed *such* an action is quite *sufficient;* at least, it would be to

Yours, &c.,

Boston, September 23rd, 1797.

DEAR FRIEND,

I set out for New York on the afternoon of the 16th. We had a pleasant journey, over a rich and well cultivated tract of country, to Bristol. We soon after crossed the Delaware, in a scow constructed to carry the stage and horses over in a few minutes, without even taking the latter from the carriage. We then entered the state of Jersey, and slept at Trenton, which we left before sunrise the next morning; a circumstance I regretted, as I wished to see the falls of the river Delaware in that neighbourhood, which I am informed are worthy the attention of a traveller.

Our journey across the Jerseys was pleasant; but the land is by no means so rich as on the other side of the Delaware. Pennsylvania is, in my opinion, justly called the Garden of America, at least of the United States *East* of the Allegany Mountains. We dined at New Brunswick, where there is a wooden bridge, with stone piers, thrown over a broad and rapid river. Our landlord informed us, several englishmen assured him, "It was *very like* Westminster Bridge. " Though my conscience would not permit me, *exactly* to chime with my countrymen, it is but justice to acknowledge, that when the infant state of the country is considered, it is a work of equal magnitude, boldly designed, and neatly executed.

About four in the afternoon, we embarked in a small vessel for New York, which is situate on an island, in a bay, formed by the conflux of two large rivers, the Hudson or North, and the East river.

The city covers the south end of the island, and, as you approach it in that direction from the Jersey shore, seems like Venice, gradually rising from the sea. The evening was uncommonly pleasant; the sky perfectly clear and serene, and the sun, in setting with all that vivid warmth of colouring peculiar to southern latitudes, illuminated some of the most beautiful scenery in nature, on the north river, and adjacent country. For some minutes all my faculties were absorbed in admiration of the surrounding objects! I never enjoyed a prospect more enchanting; but this pleasure was of short continuance; I unfortunately cast my eyes towards the city, and immediately recollected *two words* I heard in the Jerseys (yellow fever); at which the delusion vanished!

New York, Sept. 18th. —My Jersey intelligence was too true; but the disorder is chiefly confined to one part of the city, and is effectually prevented from spreading at present by the N. W. wind, which is set in this morning with uncommon severity; a circumstance which sometimes happens at this season of the year, and is of long continuance. This kind of weather the Indians call *half* winter. Unfortunately for the Philadelphians, they had no half winter in the year 1793. —I spent this day in surveying the city, which, as well as the manners of the inhabitants, is more like England than any other part of America. New York is a London in miniature, populous streets, hum of business, busy faces, shops in style, &c.

Sept. 25th, —I spent this day in viewing the city with increasing admiration: It is certainly one of the first maritime situations in the world. The extensive settlements on the banks of the Hudson, which is navigable upwards of two hundred miles, amply supplies the city with exports and provision. The inhabitants boast of having the best fish-market in the United States; their own oyster-beds, and their vicinity to the *New England states,* give them this advantage[Footnote: There are fish on the coast of America which have certain boundaries, beyond which they never go; salmon, for instance, is never found south of a river in Connecticut; and certain southern fish never visit the New England coast.].—The governor's house, new theatre, and tontine coffee house, are magnificent buildings; the public walks well laid out, and pleasantly situate.

One advantage this city possesses peculiar to itself; you may be as much in the country as you can desire for five farthings english money: the fare is no more to Long Island, where you may be conveyed, from the heart of the city, in a few minutes, and meet with as great a variety of hill and dale, wood and water, as in any part of the world. This island is ninety miles in length.

Sept. 19th. —I intended proceeding to Boston, by the way of Rhode Island, as I was informed the passage through *Hell Gates*[Footnote: A dangerous strait, between stupendous rocks.] and the Sound is very pleasant at this season; but the fear of being obliged to perform a quarantine at my arrival prevented me. I set off this morning, in the stage. Our course lay the whole length of the island, which is barren and rocky; affording some romantic situations, in several of which I observed (to use a cockney phrase) *snug little boxes*; these, I was informed, belonged to the wealthy citizens; they commanded a view of the city, the North River, the Sound, and adjacent islands.

At noon we entered Connecticut, the most southerly of the New England states. Slept at Fairfield.

On the night of the 20th we reached Hertford, the capital of the state. — About five miles from it, a house was pointed out to me, where a very shocking circumstance took place a few years ago. —A merchant, not being able to bear a change in his circumstances from affluence to extreme poverty, coolly and deliberately shot his wife and five children, and afterward himself. He tried every means, for several days, to send his wife away; but she preferred dying with him and the children. He left a paper on the table, informing his friends, that his only motive for committing this rash action was to rescue his family from a situation, which he himself found insupportable.

Sept. 21st. —We this afternoon entered the state of Massachusetts. I found New England very different from any part of America I had before seen; the soil but very indifferent, rocky, and mountainous, interspersed with some rich tracts of land in the valleys; the up lands are divided by means of stone walls, as in Derbyshire, and some other parts of Great Britain.

They have few negroes, or european emigrants; so far from wanting the latter, as in the South, they send great numbers every year to the new settlements in the South-west.

When we made any stay at a tavern on the road, I observed one of my fellow travellers (who was very eloquent upon this subject) take every opportunity of singing forth the praises of *New Virginia*[Footnote: A rich tract of country, west of the Allegany Mountains.].—The north-west wind continuing, the morning of the 22d was very cold; and we breakfasted with a number of strangers. Our orator did not lose this opportunity of holding forth on his favourite topic. I recollect the latter part of his harangue was to the following effect: — *"There, "* says he, (while the New Englanders were staring with their *mouths open,*) "when I clear a fresh lot of land on any of my plantations, I am obliged to plant it six or seven years with hemp, or tobacco, before it is sufficiently *poor* to bear wheat! My indian corn grows twelve or thirteen feet high; I'll dig four feet deep on my best land, and it shall then be sufficiently rich to *manure* your barren hills; and as to the climate, there is no comparison: this cursed cold north-west wind loses all it's severity before it reaches us; our winters are so mild, that our cattle requite no fodder, but range the woods all winter; and our summers are more moderate than on your side the Allegany; and as to— —" Here the stage-driver put an end to his oration, by informing us, all was ready to proceed on our journey.

We must not be surprised, that numbers, who cultivate an ungrateful soil in this cold climate, should be induced, by such descriptions as the above, to emigrate to our orator's land of promise, I am informed ten thousand persons emigrated from these states to Kentucky *alone*, in one year. I have lately seen a flattering description of this country, published in London: that the accounts are exaggerated, I have no doubt, as it is said to be written by a speculator; deeply interested in the sale of lands in the new settlements. I had a strong suspicion our fellow traveller was of this description, and took every opportunity to cross-examine him on this subject; he stuck true to his text, insisted that all he advanced was literally true, but acknowledged he was going to receive a sum of money for land he had sold to some emigrants from the province of Main, and that he expected to sell a considerable tract before his return. I arrived at Boston the 23d instant, four hundred and seventy-four miles from Baltimore.

Yours, &c.

P. S. I find we are to have a most vigorous theatrical opposition. A sort of dramatic mania has lately seiz'd the inhabitants. The *primitive* Bostonians would as soon have admitted the plague as a company of players; but the present inhabitants having more liberal sentiments, a company of comedians came to this town about four years ago, and ventured to exhibit dramatic pieces, under the title of *Moral Lectures*. At length a bill passed the General Assembly of Massachusetts to licence theatrical performances; and as it is natural for mankind to run from one extreme to another, they have this year *two* theatres, both of which are attended with a prodigious expence. Some of the performers are engaged at upwards of 20*l.* english per week; and Mrs. Whitlocke (sister to Mrs. Siddons, whom you may perhaps recollect at the Haymarket) is to have 180*l.* sterling for six nights. This opposition will in all probability end in the ruin of the managers, or rather of the *subscribers, who are bound for the payments.*

Boston, October 3d, 1796.

DEAR SIR,

The first leisure day after my arrival here, I went to Bunker's Hill, attended by two persons, who were spectators of the engagement, and were kind enough to point out and explain a number of particulars I wished to be acquainted with, for the purpose of enabling me to form a tolerable idea of this famous action. If general Howe meant only to give the *Yankies* a specimen of british valour, and his contempt of them and their intrenchment, he succeeded in both. —His enemies on this side the water say, "they gave him a *Rowland* for his *Oliver; that* he paid *too dear* for this victory; *that* a more prudent general would have found a better place to land the troops, and a safer mode of attack; *that* the *price* he paid for this little redoubt ought to have convinced him, he could not afford even to *bid* for Dorchester heights, if once the Americans got possession of those hills; *that* he should therefore have fortified them *himself; that——*" But as nothing is easier than to see all these *thats* when it is *too late,* I shall plague you with no more of them, but conclude with an inscription from a monument on the scene of action.

Yours, &c.

> "ERECTED, 1794,
> By King Solomon's Lodge of Free Masons,
> [Footnote: General Warren was a brother.]
> constituted at Charlestown, 1783,
> In Memory of
> MAJOR GENERAL JOSEPH WARREN,
> AND HIS BRAVE ASSOCIATES,
> Who were slain on this memorable spot,
> June 17th, 1775.

> None but they, who set a just value on the
> blessings of LIBERTY, are worthy to enjoy
> her.
> In vain we toil'd, in vain we fought,
> We bled in vain, if you, our offspring,
> Want valour to repel the assaults of her
> invaders."

CHARLES TOWN settled 1628.
———————— —burnt 1775.
———————— -- rebuilt 1776.

P. S. I was yesterday introduced to Cox, the celebrated bridge-architect: he is famous for throwing a bridge over waters, where, from the *depth* or *strength* of the current, this operation was thought impracticable. He always constructs his bridges of wood, and endeavours to give as little resistance to the water as possible: his supporters are numerous, but slender; and there is an interval between each. He tells me this idea first struck him from reading Aesop's fable of the Reed and the Oak: the reed, by *yielding*, was unhurt by a tempest, which tore up the sturdy oak by the roots.

Cox served his apprenticeship to a carpenter; and it was late in life before he attempted bridge-building. He proved his new theory on a small bridge in the country, which answering beyond his most sanguine expectations, he delivered proposals for connecting Boston to the continent, at Charleston, by means of a draw-bridge. His plan was by some supposed to proceed from a *distempered brain*. It is usual for the *ignorant* to call a projector *insane*, when his schemes exceed the bounds of *their shallow comprehensions.*

After some time, a subscription was raised; and, to the confusion of his enemies, he erected a bridge 1500 feet long, by 42 wide, where there was, at the *lowest ebb*, 28 feet of water, and the flow of the tide was from 12 to 16 feet *more*. But what is the most surprising, this bridge has stood the shock of prodigious bodies of ice, sometimes three or four feet in thickness; which are, every thaw violently forced against it with a powerful current. He was rewarded with the sum of two hundred dollars above his contract. He then went to Ireland, where he built seven bridges; the largest was at Londonderry, 1860 feet long, by 40 wide; the depth of water 37 feet, and the flow of the tide from 14 to 18 feet more. He compleated this bridge so much to the satisfaction of the gentlemen who employed him, that he was presented with a gold medal and one hundred pounds above his contract.

He speaks feelingly, and with gratitude, of the many favours he received during his residence in that kingdom.

Farewell, yours, &c.

Boston, October 9th, 1796.

DEAR FRIEND,

Boston is situate in latitude 42 deg. 23 min. north, on a small peninsula, at the bottom of Massachusetts Bay. It was built in the manner cities were in England, at the time this settlement was formed; that is to say, with, the gable end of the houses in front, the streets are narrow, ill paved, and worse lighted. But recollect, I do not include the New Town, or West Boston, in this description; which, as well as those houses that have lately been erected in the Old Town, are in the modern style.

The harbour is one of the best in the States; and, as a sea port, Boston possesses advantages superiour to any I have seen in America: being too far to the north to have any thing to fear from the worms (see a former letter from Annapolis); and so near the ocean, that the navigation is open, when the ports of Philadelphia, Baltimore, and others, three or four degrees more to the south, are entirely frozen.

Several of the public buildings are well worthy the attention of a Traveller.

The New State House will, when finished, add considerably to the beauty of the town. It is building on Beacon Hill, and commands a very extensive view of the bay of Massachusetts, and adjacent islands.

The long wharf is a bold design; it runs 1743 feet in a right line into the bay, where there is, at the lowest ebb, 17 feet of water. On this wharf are upwards of eighty large stores, containing merchandize to a great amount. I could never view these buildings without astonishment at the infatuation of the proprietors: they are, without a single exception, of *wood*, and the roofs covered with cedar shingles; were a fire to commence at either extremity with a brisk wind in the same direction, the whole must infallibly be consumed.

The new[Footnote: The *old* theatre has not been erected five years. Our opposition rages with great violence. Much ink has already been shed. One third of the public papers are crammed with what is called *Theatrical Critique*; but is in fact either the barefaced puff direct in favour of *one* theatre, or a string of abusive epithets against the *other*, equally void of truth and decency.

The dispute has lately taken *political* turn. It seems ours is the *aristocratic* theatre. The *democrats* at the New Theatre are commanded by the *Moral Lecture* manager. *Mr. Powell informs his fellow-citizens, that on Monday evening will be performed the tragedy of the Battle of Bunker's Hill.* —The English in this town affect to laugh at the eagerness with which the Bostonians swallow certain passages of this play. I laugh too, but *justice* obliges me to confess, that *John Bull* can swallow a fulsome clap trap as voraciously at any *Yankee* of them all.] theatre is a stupendous wooden building, that will contain one tenth of the inhabitants of the whole town.

The favourite promenade of the Bostonians, is the Mall, which has trees on each side, as in St. James's Park, London. This walk commands some beautiful prospects of the adjacent continent.

Immediately opposite is the village and university of Cambridge.

To open an immediate communication between Boston and the university, the New Bridge was built on the plan of Mr. Cox during his absence in Ireland; a great undertaking, including the causeways, which are covered in the same manner as the water. This bridge is within a few feet of a *mile* in length, by means of which, the bridge at Charleston, and the neck of the peninsula, our communication with the continent is so complete, that we feel but few inconveniences from our insular situation. —We have a plentiful supply of provision. Our fish-market is an excellent one: the following species are larger than I remember seeing them in Europe; viz. hallibut, cod, mackarel, smelts, and lobsters. The first is often brought to market weighing two hundred pounds. Dr. Belknap, in his History of New Hampshire, says, that when full grown, they often exceed five hundred pounds weight. The cod are from seventy to eighty pounds. Mackarel *often* exceed four, and lobsters *sometimes* thirty-five pounds weight. I have preserved a claw of one of the latter, which weighed thirty pounds: this I shall bring home with me, lest my friends should think that, in this particular, I take too liberal an advantage of the *traveller's privilege*, which I assure you I do not, when I subscribe myself

Your sincere friend.

Boston, December 27th, 1796.

DEAR FRIEND,

There is no calamity the bostonians so much, and justly dread, as fire. Almost every part of the town exhibits melancholy proofs of the devastation of that destructive element. This you will not wonder at, when I inform you that three fourths of the houses are built with *wood*, and covered with *shingles*, thin pieces of cedar, nearly in the shape, and answering the end of tiles. We have no regular fire-men, or rather mercenaries, as every master of a family belongs to a fire-company: there are several in town, composed of every class of citizens, who have entered into a contract to turn out with two buckets at the first fire alarm, and assist to the utmost of their power in extinguishing the flames, without fee or reward.

I awoke this morning about two o'clock by the cry of fire, and the jingling of all the church bells, which, with the rattling of the engines, call for water, and other *et caetera* of a bostonian fire-alarm, form a concert truly horrible.

As sleep was impossible under such circumstances, I immediately rose, and found the town illuminated. When the alarm is given at night, the female part of the family immediately place candles in the windows. This is of great service in a town where there are few lamps.

I found the fire had broken out in one of the narrow streets, and was spreading fast on all sides. I was much pleased with the regularity observed by these *amateur* fire-men. Each engine had a double row, extending to the nearest water; one row passed the full, and the other the empty buckets. The citizens not employed at the engines were pulling down the adjacent buildings, or endeavouring to save the furniture; their behaviour was bold and intrepid. The wind blew fresh at N. W.; and nothing but such uncommon exertions could possibly have saved the town, composed, as it is, of such *combustible* materials. You will naturally inquire, whether they have no other. Yes, brick and stone in great plenty; but the cheapness of a frame, or wooden building, is a great inducement for the continuance of this dangerous practice: but there is one still greater, viz. a strange idea, universal in America, that wooden houses are more healthy, and less liable to generate or retain contagious infection than those of brick or stone. This notion has been ably controverted by one of their best *writers*[Footnote: Jefferson, vicepresident of the United States.], but with little effect; and, like all other deep-rooted prejudices, will not easily be eradicated.

Your papers have, I suppose, informed you of a set of diabolical incendiaries having set fire to Savannah, Charleston, Baltimore, and New York. The villainy of these infernals is likely to be productive of some good. The inhabitants of Charleston have agreed to prohibit the erection of wooden buildings in that city. The philadelphians had before come to this prudent resolution, within certain limits, I was present when this matter was agitated. It was violently opposed by the democratic party; who insisted, that in a *free* country, a man has a right to build his house of what materials he pleases. "True, " said I, "of *stone*-brimstone —use gun-powder for lime, and mix it with spirit of turpentine, " Farewell.

Yours, &c.

P. S. I thank you for the *Apology*. It has been already twice answered in this country, or rather, the bishop has been as often abused; first, by a deist of New York, for speaking too *favourably* of the Bible; and secondly, by a hot-headed frantic of New England; who, in a work he calls *The Bible needs no Apology*, rails at his lordship for the *opposite reason*, and consigns him to eternal damnation, for *not* insisting on *every sentence* of scripture being the *inspired* word of God.

Boston, January 7th, 1797.

DEAR FRIEND,

The states of Massachusetts and Connecticut were originally settled by brownists, and other puritans, and were, for many years, an asylum for dissenters of all denominations, who fled from persecution in Europe, to exercise a still greater degree of intolerance themselves, when in power in America. You have doubtless read or heard of the *Blue* Laws of Connecticut. Without insisting on the sanguinary code, said to be formerly in force under this title, I shall briefly, and without connexion, transcribe for you some extracts from Dr. Belknap, and others of their *own* writers on this subject; on the truth of which you may rely: —

EXTRACTS.

"Severe laws, conformable to the principles of the laws of Moses, were enacted against all kinds of immorality.

"Blasphemy, idolatry, unnatural lusts, rape, murder, adultery, man-stealing, bearing false witness, rebellion against parents, were all *equally* made *capital* crimes. The law against the latter was in these words: —'If any child or children, above sixteen years of age, and of sufficient understanding, shall curse or smite their natural father or mother, he or they shall be *put to death. Exodus* xxi, 17; *Lev.* x, 9.'

"A law was passed to prohibit, under a severe penalty, the *smoking of tobacco*, which was compared to the *smoke* of the *bottomless pit. Drinking* of *healths*, and *wearing long hair*, were also forbidden, under the same penalty: the first was considered as a heathenish and idolatrous practice, grounded on the ancient libations.

"Previous to putting the laws in execution against the latter, the following proclamation was issued, and is now preserved among the records at Havard College, Cambridge, near Boston: —

"Forasmuch as the wearing of long hair, after the manner of ruffians and barbarous indians, has begun to invade New England, contrary to the rule of God's word, *Corinthians* xi, 14, which says it is a shame for a man to wear long hair; as also the commendable custom generally of all the *godly* of our nation, until these few years; we, the magistrates who have subscribed this paper, (for the showing of our own *innocency* in this behalf,) do declare and manifest our dislike and detestation against the wearing of such long hair, as against a thing *uncivil* and *unmanly*; whereby men do deform themselves, and offend *sober* and *modest* men, and do *corrupt good manners*. We do therefore, earnestly intreat all the elders of this jurisdiction, as often as they shall see cause, to *manifest their zeal* against it in their public administrations, and to take care that the *members* of their respective churches be not *defiled therewith*, that so, such as shall prove obstinate, and will not reform themselves, may have God and man to witness against them.

"The 3d month, 10th day, 1649.

"*Jo. Endicott*, Governor.
Tho. Dudley, Dep. Governor
Rich. Bellingham.
Rich. Salton Stall.
Increase Nowell.
William Hibbins.
Tho. Flint.
Rob. Bridges.
Simon Bradstreet.'

"Laws were made to regulate the intercourse between the sexes, and the advances towards matrimony. They had a ceremony of betrothing, which preceded that of marriage. *Pride* and *levity* came under the cognizance of the magistrates. Not only the richness, but the mode of dress, and cut of the hair, were subject to regulations. Women were forbidden to expose their *arms* or *bosoms* to view. It was ordered, that their sleeves should reach down to their *wrists*, and their gowns to be closed round the *neck*. Women *offending* against these laws were *presentable* by the *grand jury*.

"The following were some of their favourite arguments in favour of persecution. The celebrated Cotton, in a treatise published in 1647, laboured to prove the lawfulness of the magistrate using the civil sword, to extirpate *heretics*, from the command given to the jews, to put to death *blasphemers* and *idolaters!*

"After saying it was *toleration*, which made the world *antichristian*, he concludes his work with this singular ejaculation: —'The Lord keep us from being bewitched with the whore's cup, lest while we seem to reject her with our profession, we bring her in by a *back door* of *toleration*, and so drink deeply of the cup of the Lord's wrath, and be filled with her plagues! '

"During a war with the eastern Indians, a council was called, and a proposal made to draw upon them the *Mohawks*, their ancient enemy, though then at peace: the lawfulness of this proceeding was doubted by some *tender consciences*; but all their doubts vanished, when it was urged, that *Abraham* had entered into a confederacy with the *Amorites, among whom he dwelt*, and made use of *their* assistance in recovering his kinsman *Lot* from the hands of their *common enemy.* "

* * * * *

"The quakers at first were banished; but this proving insufficient, a succession of sanguinary laws were enacted against them; such as imprisonment, whipping, cutting off the ears, boreing the tongue with a red-hot iron, and banishment on pain of death. In consequence of these laws, four quakers were put to death at Boston only; when their friends in England procured an order from king Charles the Second, which put a stop to *capital executions.* "

And now, friend Joseph, what do you think of these primitive christians? When the *real* Christian *William Penn* arrived in America, what was *his retaliation?* He called his city *Philadelphia*, to perpetuate a memorial of the cords of peace and good will, which bound him, and all his followers, not only to one another, but even to his enemies at Boston, were they inclined to come and settle with them. —The following words of his proclamation ought to be written in letters of gold: —

"Because no people can be happy, if abridged of the freedom of their consciences, as to their religious professions and worship; I do grant and declare, that no person inhabiting this province, or territories, who shall acknowledge one Almighty God, the Creator, Ruler, and Upholder of the world, and live quietly under the civil government, shall in any case be molested, or prejudiced in his person or estate because of his conscientious persuasion or practice. "

But to return to New England; happily for these states, the revolution has done away great part of the severity of their ancient laws; but the inhabitants still retain a taste for scriptural phrases and allusions in their writings. As you are fond of *poetry*, I send you two specimens of this kind of writing; the first is from a tomb-stone at *Plymouth*[Footnote: The oldest settlement north of Virginia.]. It was written by one of the first settlers, and is in the true spirit of those times. —

EPITAPH UPON GENERAL ATHERTON.

"Here lies our captain, and major,
  Of Suffolk was withal,
A *godly* magistrate was he,
  And major general.
Two troops of horse came here,
  (Such love his worth did crave;)
Ten companies of foot also,
  Mourning, marched to his grave.
Let all that read be sure to keep
  The *faith, as he has done.*
He lives now *crowned* with *Christ*;
  His name was Humphrey Atherton."

In order to understand the second, I must inform you, it is usual for boys, who expect christmas boxes, to present their masters' customers with a copy of verses, expressive of their good wishes, &c. The call-boy of the theatre, (a mechanic's son of this town,) had the following *verses* written in the usual style by the *poet* commonly employed on these occasions, and when printed, delivered one to each of the performers. —

"THE CALL-BOY OF THE THEATRE,
FEDERAL-STREET,
NEW YEAR'S WISH, 1797.

"Look up, worthy friends, from yonder bright hills
  See how Phoebus smiles, to hail the new year:
I bring you a tribute—rejoice thus to find,
  So many are living, and meet with us here.

"May health be confirm'd, and sickness remov'd;
  May no sweeping flames take place in this state;
We sympathise deeply with neighbouring friends,
  Whose cup has run over with this bitter fate.

"May *teachers* this day find *help from above*
  To publish glad news, as *heralds of grace,*
While *Zion* is mourning her light shall break forth,
  And shadows of midnight away from her chase.

"I wish through this year *God's presence* may smile
  On all your just schemes at home or abroad;
I wish you his protection, by sea or by land;
  May your *theatrical works* find favour in *God.*
[Footnote: The boy must surely mean the *gods.*]

"Gentlemen and ladies, accept these wishes sincere,
  And I wish you all a happy new year."

Boston, January 1st, 1797.

DEAR FRIEND,

To answer your last, wherein you desire me to send you the exact state of negro slavery in this country, is a task to which I am unequal.

You will conceive the great difficulty of obliging you in this request, when you are informed, that on this subject each individual state has it's own laws. The only point in which they are unanimous, is to prohibit their importation, either from the Coast of Africa, or the West Indies. I can only inform you in general terms, that in the *southern states* there is little alteration in the negro code since the revolution; of course the laws are nearly the same as in the British West India islands. In the *middle states*, though negro slavery is allowed, their situation has been considerably meliorated, by a variety of laws in their favour, some tending to their gradual emancipation, others to render their servitude less irksome, &c.

Societies are formed in several of the large towns to enforce these lenient laws, and to purchase the freedom of a few of the most deserving slaves. The quakers, beside liberating all their negroes, have contributed liberally towards the funds these societies have established, for carrying their benevolent intentions into effect. In consequence of these measures, there are a number of free negroes in Philadelphia, whose situation is very comfortable. A handsome episcopalian church has been built for their use, and one of the most respectable negroes ordained, who performs all the duties of his office with great solemnity and fervour of devotion, assisted occasionally by his white brethren; and there are also two schools, where the children of people of colour are educated gratis; one supported by the quakers, the other by the abolition society.

Negro slavery, under any modification or form, is prohibited in this state (Massachusetts,) also in New Hampshire, the province of Maine, and, *I believe*, in all the *New England states.*

As to your other queries respecting the negroes, I send you my sentiments, infinitely better expressed by Jefferson, notwithstanding all that Imlay, Wilberforce, and other authors, have written against his assertion, viz., that "Negroes are *inferiour* to the whites, both in the endowments of *body* and *mind.* " I am clearly and decidedly of his opinion. A strict attention to this subject, during three years residence in these states, has convinced me of the truth of every tittle of the following extract from his Virginia, which I enclose for your perusal, and am, most sincerely,

Yours, &c.

"The first difference that strikes us is colour. Whether the black of the negro reside in the reticular membrane, between the skin and scarf skin, or in the scarf skin itself; whether it proceed from the colour of the blood, the colour of the bile, or from that of some other secretion, the difference is fixed in nature, and is as real as if it's seat and cause were better known to us. And is this difference of no importance? Is it not the foundation of a greater or less share of beauty in the two races? Are not the fine mixtures of red and white, the expression of every passion by a greater or less suffusion of colour in the one, preferable to that eternal monotony, that immovable veil of black, which covers all the emotions of the other race? Add to these, flowing hair, a more elegant symmetry of form, their own judgment in favour of the whites, declared by their preference to them, as uniformly as is the preference of the oroonowtang for the black women over those of his own species? The circumstance of superiour beauty is thought worthy attention in the propagation of our horses, dogs, and other domestic animals; why not in that of man?

"Beside those of colour, figure, and hair, there are other physical distinctions, proving a difference of race. They have less hair on the face and body. They secrete less by the kidneys, and more by the glands of the skin; which gives them a very strong and disagreeable odour. This greater degree of transpiration renders them more tolerant of heat, and less so of cold, than the whites. Perhaps a difference of structure in the pulmonary aparatus, which a late ingenious experimentalist, (Crawford) has discovered to be the principal regulator of animal heat, may have disabled them from extricating, in the act of inspiration, so much of that fluid from the outer air; or obliged them, in expiration, to part with more of it.

"They seem to require less sleep. A black, after hard labour through the day, will be induced by the slightest amusement, to sit up till midnight, or later, though knowing he must be out with the dawn of the morning. They are at least as brave, and more adventurous; but this may proceed from want of forethought, which prevents their seeing a danger till it be present; when present, they do not go through it with more coolness and steadiness than the whites. They are more ardent after the female; but love seems with them more an eager desire, than a tender delicate mixture of sentiment and sensation. Their griefs are transient. Those numberless afflictions which render it doubtful, whether Heaven has given life to us more in mercy, or in wrath, are less felt and sooner forgotten with them. In general, their existence appears to participate more of sensation than reflection. To this must be ascribed their disposition to sleep, when abstracted from their diversions, or unemployed in labour. An animal, whose body is at rest, and who does not reflect, must be disposed to sleep of course. Comparing them by their faculties of memory, reason, and imagination, it appears to me that in memory, they are equal to the whites; in reason much inferiour. As I think one could scarcely be found capable of tracing, and comprehending the investigations of Euclid; and that in imagination they are dull, tasteless, and anomalous. It would be unfair to follow them to Africa for this investigation. We will consider them here, on the same stage with the whites. And where the facts are not apocryphal on which a judgment is to be formed, it will be right to make allowances for the difference of condition, of conversation, and of the sphere in which they move. Many millions of them have been brought to, and born in America. Most of them indeed have been confined to tillage, to their own homes, and their own society; yet many have been so situate, that they might have availed themselves of the conversation of their masters; many have been brought up to the handicraft arts, and from that circumstance have always been associated with the whites; some have been liberally educated, and all have lived in countries where the arts and sciences are cultivated to a considerable degree, and have had before their eyes samples of the best work from abroad. The Indians with no advantages of this kind, will often carve figures on their pipes, not destitute of merit and design. They will crayon out an animal, a plant, or a country, so as to prove the existence of a germe in their minds, which only wants cultivation. They astonish you with strokes of the most sublime oratory, such as prove their reason and sentiment strong, their imagination glowing and elevated; but never yet could I find a black, that had uttered a thought above the level of plain narration[Footnote: "Sleep hab no massa, " was the answer of a sleepy negro, who was told that his massa called him. —See Edward's History of Jamaica, 2d Vol.]; never see even an elementary trait of painting, or sculpture. In music they are more generally gifted than the whites with accurate ears for tune, and time; and they have been found capable of imagining a small catch[Footnote: "The instrument proper to them is the *banjore*, which they brought here from Africa, and which is the origin of the guitar, it's chords being precisely the four lower chords of that instrument. " J—— N.]. Whether they will be equal to the composition of a more extensive run of melody, or of complicated harmony[Footnote: From this circumstance, I conceive our author's *catch* was improperly so called.], is yet to be proved. Misery is often the parent of the most affecting touches in poetry. Among the blacks is misery enough, God knows, but no poetry. Love is the peculiar oestrum of the poet: their love is ardent; but it kindles the senses only, not the imagination. Religion, or rather fanaticism, has produced a *Phyllis Wheatly*; but it could not produce a poet. Ignatius Sancho has approached nearer to merit in composition; yet his letters do more credit to the heart than the head; supposing them to have been genuine, and to have received amendment from no other hand; points which would not be easy of investigation. The improvement of the blacks in body and mind, in the first instance of their mixture with the whites, has been observed by every one, and proves their inferiority is not the effect merely of their condition in life.

"The white slaves, among the Romans, were often their rarest artists; they excelled too in science, insomuch as to be usually employed as tutors to their masters' children. Epictetus, Terence, and Phoedrus, were slaves. Whether further observation will, or will not, verify the conjecture, that Nature has been less bountiful to them, in the endowments of the head, I believe in those of the heart she will be found to have done them justice. That disposition to theft, with which they have been branded, must be ascribed to their situation, and not to any depravity of the moral sense. The man, in whose favour no laws of property exist, probably feels himself less bound to respect those made in favour of others. When arguing for ourselves, we lay it down as a fundamental, that laws, to be just, must give a reciprocation of right; that without this, they are mere arbitrary rules of conduct, founded in force, and not in conscience. And it is a problem which I give the master to solve, whether the religious precepts against the violation of property, were not formed for *him*, as well as his slave, and whether the slave may not as justifiably take a little from one who has taken *all* from him, as he would slay one that would slay him?

"That a change in the relation in which a man is placed should change his ideas of moral right and wrong, is neither new, nor confined to the blacks; Homer tells us, it was so 2600 years ago: —

89

'Jove fixed it certain, that whatever day makes a man a slave, takes half his worth away. ' But the slaves Homer speaks of were whites.

"But to return to the blacks. Notwithstanding this consideration, which must weaken their respect for the laws of property, we find among them numerous instances of the most rigid integrity; and as many as among their better instructed masters, of benevolence, gratitude, and unshaken fidelity.

"The opinion that they are inferiour in the faculties of reason and imagination, must be hazarded with great diffidence. To justify a general conclusion requires many observations, even where the subject may be submitted to the anatomical knife, to optical glasses, to analysis by fire or solvents: how much more, then, when it is a faculty, not a substance, we are examining; where it eludes the research of all the senses; where the conditions of it's existence are various, and variously combined; where the effects of those which are present or absent bid defiance to calculation; let me add too, in a circumstance where our conclusions would degrade a whole race of men from the rank in the scale of beings, which their Creator may perhaps have given them! To our reproach it must be said, though for a century and a half we have had under our eyes the races of black and red men, they have never yet been viewed by us as subjects of natural history. I advance it therefore as a suspicion only, that the blacks[Footnote: Where Jefferson makes use of the word *Black*, in this extract, it is rigidly confined to the *Negroes* originally from the coast of Africa, or their descendants.], whether originally a distinct race, or made so by time and circumstances, are inferiour to the whites in the endowments both of body and mind. "

Boston, December 29th, 1796.

DEAR FRIEND,

Upon my arrival here, I had once more the mortification to find myself in the neighbourhood of the yellow fever, which had lately been imported. The uncommon, early, and severe north-west winds entirely prevented it from spreading; a fortunate circumstance for the inhabitants of Boston, as, from the narrowness of their streets, great population, and other circumstances, it must have been very fatal, had it not been by this means destroyed.

In order to give you the most regular account of this disorder I could procure, I must repeat several circumstances from former letters.

The yellow fever, which has lately been so fatal, is a *new disorder*, first brought to the West Indies, in a slave-ship from the coast of Africa, late in the year 1792. It spread rapidly from island to island, and in July, 1793, was first imported to the continent in a french schooner to Philadelphia. The physicians of that city, naturally concluding it was the usual yellow fever of the West Indies, applied the common remedies in that case: viz., bark, and other astringents. In nine cases out of ten, death was the inevitable consequence to all who took these medicines. The disease was equally fatal to the faculty. A universal despondency took place, till doctor Rush, suspecting this was a new disorder, applied an opposite method of cure, by mercurial medicines, and copious bleedings; which, when administered in the first or second stage of the disorder, had the desired effect.

I send you an extract from the doctor's pamphlet, wherein he explains his motives for adopting this method of cure, &c.

Speaking of the effect of the lancet, he says, "It was at this time my old master reminded me of Dr. Sydenham's remark, that *moderate* bleeding did harm in the plague, where *copious* bleeding was indicated, and that, in the cure of that disorder, we should leave Nature wholly to herself, or take the cure altogether out of her hands. "

The truth of this observation was obvious: —By taking away as much blood as restored the blood-vessels to a morbid degree of action, without reducing this action afterward, pain, congestion, and inflammation, were greatly increased; all of which were prevented, or occurred in a less degree, when the system rose gradually from the state of depression which had been induced by indirect debility. Under the influence of the facts and reasonings which have been mentioned, I bore the same testimony in acute cases against what was called *moderate* bleeding, that I did against bark, wine, and laudanum, in this fever. —I drew from many persons seventy or eighty ounces of blood in five days.

* * * * *

After the cold weather had completely destroyed this disorder, it did not appear again in the United States till the next year, when it was imported to Baltimore and New Haven; a distance from each other of more than five hundred miles. The cold weather again destroyed it, till carried, in 1795, to Charleston and New York, equally distant from each other; and this summer it was imported to Charleston, New York, Boston, and Newbery Port; a distance of one thousand five hundred miles along the coast; but fortunately the early N. W. winds destroyed it in all these places before it had made any considerable progress.

A quarantine upon vessels from the infected islands would effectually prevent the importation of this plague; but if performed in the *literal sense of the word,* it would materially hurt the West India trade of the Americans.

You have little to fear from this disorder being brought to England; experience has clearly proved, this fever cannot exist in a *cold* climate; but was it to be imported to the south of Europe, the consequences would be dreadful indeed. I before told you, the negroes were not afflicted with the yellow fever, though universally employed as nurses to the sick.

A disease that will affect but *one* species of men is not new. About the year 1652, a very dreadful and uncommon plague ravaged this part of America, and actually extirpated several nations of the Indians, without, in a single instance, affecting the *white* emigrants, though continually among them. This strange circumstance the fanatics of New England accounted for in their usual way, as appears from several of their sermons, still preserved: —

"It was a just judgment of God upon these heathenish and idolatrous nations; the Lord took this method of destroying them, that he might make the more room for his *chosen people.* " A *philosopher* would perhaps demand a better reason. Apropos of philosophers—An american writer has been endeavouring to investigate the age of the world, from the *Falls of Niagara!* According to *his* calculation (which, by the by, is not a little curious) it is *36960* years since the first rain fell upon the face of the earth!

Yours, &c.

Boston, December 19th, 1796.

DEAR SIR,

I before hinted to you, that the Americans pay very little attention to their fisheries.

Exclusive of the shad fishery, which is only two months in the year, there is not *one* individual, either in the city of Philadelphia, or it's vicinity, who procures a livelihood by catching fish in the Delaware, though that river abounds with sturgeon, perch, cat-fish, eels, and a vast variety of others, which would meet with a sure sale in the Philadelphia markets: but this is a trifle to their neglect of the greatest fishery in the universe; for such certainly is that on the banks of Newfoundland.

The Americans now being at peace with most of the piratical states of Barbary, will find an excellent market for their fish in the Mediterranean. This circumstance may induce congress to pay some attention to the hints thrown out by Dr. Belknap, in his Account of the American Newfoundland Fishery, which I transcribe for you perusal: —

"The cod-fishery is either carried on by boats or schooners. The boats in the winter season go out in the morning, and return at night. In the spring they do not return till they are filled. The schooners make three trips to the banks of Newfoundland in a season; the first, or spring cargo, are large, thick fish, which, after being properly salted and dried, are kept alternately above and under ground, till they become so mellow as to be denominated *dumb fish*. These, when boiled, are red, and of an excellent quality; they are chiefly consumed in these states. The fish caught in the other two trips, during the summer and fall, are white, thin, and less firm; these are exported to Europe and the West Indies; they are divided into two sorts; one called merchantable, and the other Jamaica fish.

"The places where the cod-fishery is chiefly carried on, are the Isle of Shoals, Newcastle, Rye, and Hampton. The boats employed in this fishery are of that light and swift kind called whale-boats; they are rowed either with two or four oars, and steered with another; and being equally sharp at each end, move with the utmost celerity on the surface of the ocean. The schooners are from twenty to fifty tons, carry six or seven men, and one or two boys. When they make a tolerable voyage, they bring over five or six hundred quintals of fish, salted and stowed in bulk. At their arrival, the fish is rinced in salt water, and spread on hurdles composed of brush-wood, and raised on stakes three or four feet from the ground. They are kept carefully preserved from the rain: they should not be wet from the time they are first spread on the hurdle till they are boiled for the table.

"This fishery has not of late years been prosecuted with the same spirit it was fifty or sixty years ago, when the shores were covered with fish-flakes, and seven or eight ships were annually loaded for Spain or Portugal, beside what was carried to the West Indies. Afterward they found it more convenient to cure the fish at Corscaw, which was nearer to the banks. It was continued there to great advantage till 1744, when it was broken up by the french war. After the peace it revived, but not in so great a degree as before. Fish was frequently cured in the summer on the eastern shores and islands, and in the spring and fall at home.

"Previously to the late revolution the greater part of remittances were made to Europe by the fishery; but it has not yet recovered from the shock which it received by the war with Britain: it is however in the power of the Americans to make more advantage of the cod-fishery perhaps than, any of the european nations. We can fit out vessels at less expense, and by reason of the westerly winds, which prevail on our coasts in February and March, can go to the banks earlier in the season than the Europeans, and take the best fish. We can dry it in a clearer air than the foggy shores of Newfoundland and Nova Scotia. We can supply every necessary from among ourselves; vessels, spars, sails, cordage, anchors, lines, hooks, and provision. Salt can be imported from abroad cheaper than it can be made at home, if it be not too much loaded with duties. Men can always be had to go on shares, which is by far the most profitable way, both to the employer and fisherman. The fishing banks are an inexhaustible source of wealth; and the fishing business is a most excellent nursery for seamen; it therefore deserves every encouragement and indulgence from an enlightened and rational legislature. "

Boston, March 4th, 1797.

DEAR FRIEND,

Being very busy in making preparation for my voyage to England, I have not leisure to write you a long epistle, but enclose you one I sent to an american friend in the south. —Farewell.

This will most likely be the last letter you will receive from me on this side of the Atlantic. The French have already taken two hundred sail of american vessels. I hope my next may not be dated from *Brest*.

To Mr. — — — —,

State of— — — —.

DEAR SIR,

In consequence of my promise at parting, I sit down to give you some account of *Yankee Land*. You were perfectly right in telling me I should find the New England states very different from your part of America.

The first object that would strike you is the population of the country. In one day's journey through Connecticut, I saw as many towns, villages, and houses, as I ever remember seeing, when travelling the same distance in England; a prospect you *Buck-skins* can have no idea of.

The next is the beauty of the women, (I beg their pardon; that would be the *first* object that would strike *you!*) Their great superiority in that respect may be accounted for, from their being of *engllsh* descent. Your women have not all that *advantage*, ('True english prejudice this! ' methinks I hear you mutter): great part are of *dutch*, or *german* descent. The close iron stoves they have introduced among you are terrible enemies to beauty. Why you so obstinately persist in a custom so prejudicial to health, I cannot imagine. Your plea, that the coldness of the climate makes them indispensable, I can-not admit of; you know, that we are here three degrees to the north of you, and that the present is the coldest winter since the year 1780-81; and yet I have not seen a close stove since I left New York. The tavern bills in these states are near one hundred per cent under yours. The exorbitant charges of your tavern-keepers are a disgrace to the country: I could never account for your submitting so quietly to their impositions.

Whether it be owing to the abolition of negro slavery, and the sale of irish, and german redemptioners, (which, by the by, is nearly as bad, and ought not to be tolerated in a free country,) or to the great population, or to the produce of the land being of less value than in the south: I say whether it be owing to any, or to all of these causes, I know not; but certain it is, a greater strain of industry runs through all ranks of people than with you; and it is equally certain, that the lower order of citizens receive a better education, and of course are more intelligent, and better informed. This you will not wonder at, when I tell you there are seven free schools in Boston, containing about nine hundred scholars, and that in the country schools are in a still greater proportion. They are maintained by a tax on every class of citizens, therefore education may be claimed by *all* as a *right*.

This climate is much colder, compared with yours, than I can account for geographically; but it may perhaps be owing to our having a greater proportion of easterly winds, which, coming immediately from the banks of Newfoundland, are attended with a cloudy sky, and thick atmosphere. These may tend to mitigate the heats of summer, but are very disagreeable in the other seasons. The coldness of the climate is plainly to be perceived in the birch tree, which is here common in the woods; and the *want* of the mocking bird, the red bird, and a great variety of others, that visit you in the glimmer from South America. The fox squirrel too is scarce, and the gray squirrel almost white. We cannot cultivate the sweet, or tropical potatoe, but import it from Carolina. Even the peach is late, small, and acid. The coldness of the climate, and the fanaticism of the inhabitants, make the New England states by no means such desirable places of residence, as those of the south, to

Yours, &c.

Dover, April 22nd, 1797.

DEAR FRIEND,

On the 12th of March I embarked in the Betsy, captain Hart, for London; my live stock consisted of some fowls, four brace of partridges, a flying squirrel, and a young racoon. We sailed about midnight, with a good breeze at S. W., and were in a few hours clear of the land.

On the evening of the 13th, we met with a hard gale at N. E. by N. — The degree of cold was intolerable. We shipped some heavy seas, and our rigging being intirely incrusted with ice, our captain was resolved to stand to the south, in search of better weather. The next morning being on the edge of the gulf stream, we were witness to a strange struggle between the warmth of the current, and the coldness of the surrounding ocean and atmosphere: the stream actually smoaked like a caldron! We ran as far to the south as latitude 38, when the wind shifting to the S. W., in a few hours we found a wonderful change of climate: the degree of heat was, at least, equal to that of a usual summer day in England, without the disagreeable pressure experienced from a thick atmosphere. The air was perfectly clear, elastic, and animating, nothing could be more charming; but this was of short continuance; the next morning the wind shifted to the N. E., and blew a *gale*, which lasted eighteen hours. We had then a calm, which was succeeded by westerly winds,

On the 27th, we had run down half our longitude, four degrees of which we sailed in the last twenty four hours.

On the 29th, we met with another very severe gale at E. N.E., which soon obliged us to strike our top-gallant-yards, and lie too, under our mizen and mizen stay sail. During the confusion of the night, my racoon got loose, and found means to kill all my partridges! and, as misfortunes seldom come alone; a large spanish cat we had on board, caught my flying squirrel. The loss of my partridges was the more provoking, as they were in perfect health, and I had no doubt of landing them safe: so ends my project of propagating the breed of these birds in England.

In a former letter, wherein I gave you my motives for making this attempt, I mentioned their extreme hardiness; of this I had now additional proofs: these birds were in a coop on the deck, and I expected every sea we shipped over our quarter during the first gale, they certainly would be drowned; but was agreeably surprised, when the gale was over, to find them very little the worse for their severe ducking.

April 14th. —For the last eight days we have been beating against an easterly wind, a few leagues to the westward of the chops of the channel, subject to continual alarms from french cruisers, of all situations the most disagreeable. This evening we had soundings at 80 fathom, and a favourable change of the wind to the westward.

On the 15th we saw an american-built ship standing athwart us, by her course and appearance evidently a french prize, bound to Brest. She had her anchors over her bows, and most likely had been but a few days from some port in St. George's Channel. About five hours after we were boarded by the Spitfire, british sloop of war; we informed the lieutenant of the exact course of the prize, and he immediately gave chace.

The next day we made the Bill of Portland. Our passage up the channel was very pleasant, till within six leagues of Dover, when we once more encountered a violent easterly gale, which, for the fifth time, reduced us to our courses. Night coming on, and not being able to procure a pilot, we were a little uneasy. The gale abating the next day, a pilot came on board. He had the conscience to demand three guineas to put me on shore! but took one third of the sum, which I think he deserved, as we were six hours making this harbour. I found the custom house officers, and their myrmidon porters, exactly as Smollet has described them; two of these *gentlemen* had the impudence to charge me half a guinea for bringing my trunk seventy yards. —So ends my tour. I am once more landed in Old England, after an absence of three years and nine months, with a plentiful lack of money and *some* experience! —

Farewell.

Yours, &c.

THE END.

Printed in the United Kingdom
by Lightning Source UK Ltd.
135145UK00001B/306/P